The Trouble with Horses

Ulrik Schramm

Translated by Chris Belton

J. A. Allen
London

British Library Cataloguing in Publication Data

Schramm, Ulrik.
  The trouble with horses.
  1. Livestock: horses. Training
  I. Title   II. (Die untungenden des Pferdes.
  English)
  636.1'083

  ISBN 0–85131–457–0

Title of the original German edition:
DIE UNTUGENDEN DES PFERDES
© 1986 BLV Verlagsgesellschaft mbH, München

Published in Great Britain by
J. A. Allen & Company Limited,
1, Lower Grosvenor Place, Buckingham Palace Road,
London, SW1W 0EL

Printed in Great Britain

Contents

Equine Behaviour Problems

Introduction

Ever increasing numbers of books are available on the subject of horse and rider training. These books are based on various different systems, approaches and philosophies originating in early or in more recent times. The study of equine psychology, however, is of relatively modern origin, in spite of the fact that when a problem situation arises, it is the horse's psyche which is at the root of the problem. Knowledge of horse psychology comes instinctively to a good trainer or horsemaster who possesses 'horse sense', that is, a 'feeling' for how the horse feels and 'thinks'. However, many people who own or work with horses are thoughtless and unintentionally cruel to the animal on which they make so many demands. It is less a question of brutality – although that exists too – than of kindness unsupported by reason.

Thoughtlessness is the cause of animal suffering far more often than we tend to think. The horse kept as a riding animal in today's conditions is treated all too often with a lack of consideration which takes the most absurd and inconceivable forms. The aim of this study is to create a better understanding of equine behaviour by examining why our horses react in such and such a way. In fact most equine behaviour problems and resistances are the result of mistakes on *our* part. Fear, inability to comply and failure to understand what is required are all too often the reasons for the horse doing the wrong thing and for the associated behaviour problems, as are impatience and asking too much or too soon.

Spohr has drawn up a few guidelines which are worth mentioning in this respect: 'Handle your horse kindly and as frequently as possible. Be nice to him when you go up to him and when you leave him. If you must punish him, do so firmly, or even sharply if appropriate, but never act in anger or with uncontrolled violence. Punishment must always be followed by reconciliation. Do not allow anyone else to treat your horse unkindly, least of all his groom'.

E. F. Seidler wrote: 'Every horse must be treated differently, in accordance with its own peculiarities'. Another quote, from V. Krane, underlines one of the most important principles of horse training: 'It is the many small victories we achieve which develop the habit of obedience'.

We must bear in mind that the horse is by nature a very active animal, and is particularly adept at running for long distances and at manoeuvring at speed. The horse falls into the category of 'creatures of flight', but it is the pleasure which it takes in movement which is its most noteworthy characteristic. This feature has been developed over millions of years of the horse's evolutionary history. Another characteristic which has been important in the horse's development is its ability to adapt to its environment. The horse is found almost all over the world, and only the ice in the north and tsetse fly in the south have stood in its way. The ability to adapt to extreme climatic conditions is connected with a high degree of skin activity. The horse's enormous capacity for sweating (which is greater than that of any other animal) is a sign of this. The sensitivity of the horse is also related to this skin activity. The closeness of the nerves to the surface explains the horse's ability to respond to the most minute stimuli, a characteristic for which it is well known. Another essential feature of the horse is the many facets of its behaviour; no other animal has such a wide range of physical and mental activity.

The modern horse is the result of a very long period of evolution, which began more than sixty million years ago in the Eocene period, long before man came into existence. The first traces of *Eohippus* show that the ancestor of the modern horse was a creature the size of a fox. It had four toes on its front feet and three on its hind, and increased in size, strength and speed by a process of adaptation to its environment until it reached its present-day specifications. It is still not known where the development of this creature of the Tertiary period actually began, since finds have been made in both London and North America (Wyoming, the Watsatch and Wind River basins). As the climate became colder over the course of the Tertiary period and grass steppes appeared, the ground also became firmer, and *Eohippus* adapted to the changes in its environment. It became a grazing animal, its jaws and teeth altered, the middle toe became larger, and it lost a toe on its fore feet reducing the number to three. It engaged in long migrations across the interconnected continents of Eurasia and North America, increasing all the time in size and speed, and became a steppe dweller and a creature of flight.

After many millions of years, owing to changes in climatic conditions, different family branches developed, retrogression took place and certain families died out. The Ice Age saw the development of the species with which man was to come into contact later, in the Quartenary period. During this period of the horse's evolution the side toes had disappeared and the incisor teeth had developed the flat surfaces which are now so important in assessing the age of the horse. *Eohippus* had evolved into *Equus caballus*. The final stage in this evolution of the wild horse still has its living representatives in the form of *Equus Przewalski*.

The horse's first encounter with man was that of a wild animal with a hunter. Later, man followed the herds around nomad-style, killing what he needed for food and clothing. Then he learnt how to manage the herd, and began a process of selection. The last remaining wild horses still living in the wild are in Central Asia, on the border between China and Mongolia. The Soviet Union is endeavouring to bring these few remaining specimens into a reserve where they will be safe from persecution by man.

We should always bear in mind these sixty million years and more of evolution when we discuss the horse's behaviour; they provide the basis for understanding this behaviour. Not only do they enable us to understand the horse's reactions, but they help us avoid nasty accidents which are sometimes a consequence of these reactions, for example, the injuries which can result from kicking, shying and bolting. We shall have more success in training and handling horses if we consider them intelligently than if we see them as objects which we can treat as we please.

So we have a horse, just one product of this long evolutionary process, in our stables. It does not matter whether it is a thoroughbred or a cob; breed and colour are irrelevant, because the patterns of behaviour are more or less the same. Years ago, horses performed the duties now taken over by the motor car, and people either rode or went by carriage to get from one place to another. The lives of people and horses were therefore more closely linked, with a greater contact between man and horse. Horse knowledge was handed down from one generation to the next, and was derived from knowledge of the job the horse was required to do. Nowadays the horse is, for many people, nothing more than a piece of apparatus which they use, either inconsiderately or downright brutally, to perform their sport. Town dwellers, even in provincial areas, will, because of their lack of experience, need to acquire some knowledge of horse psychology to protect themselves and their horses from the consequences of the horse doing the wrong thing and of the resulting vices.

First of all we must define what is good and what is bad behaviour in the horse. Good and bad do not necessarily have the same meaning for a horse as they do for a person. If we start with the premise that the horse is essentially good-natured, this leads us to conclude that any 'viciousness' is the result of three phenomena: temperament, instinct and upbringing. A horse does not start off vicious, it becomes vicious as the result of incorrect treatment. The horse's sensitivity is in itself a potential source of problems: a painful mouth or teeth, pressure from the saddle or girth, girthing up too tightly, saddling up wrongly or in haste and not taking enough care with the training, will all cause the horse to react accordingly, as will brutality, rough treatment and impatience on the part of the rider. Worst of all are unjust punishments; all resistances are caused by discomfort and pain, and a horse cannot, and must not, be punished for pain! As for rough treatment, horses do not understand it as a punishment, but as hostile behaviour. It causes them to stop listening and to defend themselves all the more, in other words, the resistance grows from within.

Observation and knowledge of how the horse's mind works is very beneficial for both horse and rider. G. Steinbrecht wrote: 'Correct understanding of the mental qualities of the horse and their expression, and the ability, based on this knowledge, to influence them is essential, and becomes even more so as we become involved with more advanced training. Correct assessment of temperament and an insight into the horse's nature are just as essential for success as correct assessment of its physical qualities'. Although these remarks referred mainly to training, they are equally relevant to the handling of the horse in general. Any sensitive, observant rider will, with a little thought, be able to formulate his own knowledge on the subject. This process reflects one of the principal methods of animal psychology: self-observation or 'introspection', whereby certain elements of equine behaviour are perfectly comprehensible to man. This does not mean that we must judge the horse in human terms, but rather we should consider the analogies and dissimilarities, and use them as a basis for studying and understanding the horse's behaviour.

The horse's powers of thought and its ability to draw conclusions are relatively limited in comparison with those of other domestic animals. Its reactions can be understood with reference to the lifestyle of its ancestors (creatures of flight). However, equine nature does have some noteworthy characteristics: the horse has an incredibly good memory, a highly developed sense of direction, a pronounced herd instinct, a dependence on habit, and an extremely discerning sense of smell. It is also a gregarious animal, with a dependence on others of its kind and a marked need for friendship; it is very sensitive to good treatment, praise and reproaches, it is ambitious and a courageous fighter. Máday says that the horse can also reason, but adds: 'whether it actually has ideas and forms judgements and conclusions has not been established because these activities have not yet been precisely explored and defined'. Yet the horse does form simple ideas and judgements, and in some cases it even displays the rudiments of an ability to draw conclusions. Horses know how to simulate (e.g. lameness). In cavalry stables there were frequent cases of horses which regularly rubbed off their headcollars, waited until the guard had passed, and then went looking for food or to visit a friend.

The horse's ability to express its feelings is well known. Although many riders do not notice it, the play of the horse's features is far from invisible. The eyes, for example, are capable of a wide range of expressions. A calm horse has a different look in its eyes than a frightened one. Trust is also expressed in the eyes, as are attentiveness and willingness or indifference. Everyone knows that blank look on the face of the exhausted horse which has been plodding around for hours on end with one riding school pupil after another on its back; and the resistance of the horse which has been unreasonably asked to do things of which it is incapable, either because it has been overstretched or because it does not understand.

The nostrils and mouth also play their part in these expressions. There is Flehmen's posture, yawning, baring the teeth, and the pendulous lower lip of the weary horse. Neighing and snorting also have a wider range of expression than is generally thought. Horses are the only animals which can show their feelings in this way: these vocal expressions can be used to convey fear, excitement or surprise, and they can either be used in play or as a warning. Mares in particular (though geldings too), have a wider range of 'neighs' than stallions.

The play of a horse's ears is another form of expression. The ears can show attentiveness, unwillingness, willingness or menace. Other means of expression are the mouth (e.g. baring the teeth), the fore feet (stamping, pawing), the hind feet and the tail. Moreover, the physiologists claim that the horse always looks in the direction that its ears point.

In yawning (*above*) the mouth is opened and the eyes half-shut, while in Flehmen's posture (*below*) the mouth remains shut and the eyes are open.

The horse is an extraordinarily sensitive animal which feels things very strongly, and it uses these forms of expression reflexively to communicate with its fellows, and also with man. For this reason, man should learn to understand this language. Horses are also very sensitive to noise, although this does not prevent them from making a loud noise themselves, for example kicking the sides of the box at feed time. When working a horse or working in the stables, one should be as quiet as possible, and not shout or scream. In certain circumstances, a loud rebuke will be received as a more severe punishment than a blow. Being spoken to quietly is a pleasant experience for a horse, speaking to it in a monotone has a calming effect, whereas the actual words are irrelevant: 'it is the tone which makes the music'. Music, too, without loud, sharp accents, calms the horse, though certain types of rhythms can have an exciting effect. It must be added, though, that it is not true that horses adapt to and follow the beat of the music when performing trot, passage etc. In fact it is the rider who unconsciously keeps with the beat or tries to go with it. In the circus the band usually has great difficulty in keeping in time with the horses in the liberty acts.

Horses learn certain words very fast. A loud 'No!', and 'Good boy' spoken in a different tone of voice are not the only expressions the horse can recognise. In fact it can understand a wide range of words, even when they are heard nearby as opposed to being addressed directly to it. Riders will often find that their horses break into canter by themselves when the other riders in the school are told to 'canter on'.

Spohr remarks: 'The person who attempts to correct a horse which is playing up without using his voice will succeed only with difficulty'. The number of tones of voice, and of categories of tones, which the horse can distinguish between is probably much larger than we think. It understands them particularly well when they are accompanied by visual or tactual signs.

The horse's hearing reacts with extraordinary sensitivity to nuances of tones. For this reason, 'conversation' with the horse should be considered a psychological means of communicating with it. We should talk to our horses when we are working them and when we are handling them in the stable. They will become more attentive, they will focus their attention on this contact, and their intelligence will develop. Hence, the tone of voice, as has already been said, should be calm, even cajoling, as if speaking to a child. For admonishments, encouragement and reprimands, a different tone of voice is required.

It should be mentioned in this connection that the horse can definitely reason, and that its capacity for so doing is certainly not related to its level of 'breeding'. Reason, in this sense, is not the ability to work things out or think abstractly; with the horse it is more a capacity for 'forming conceptions from sensations received in a state of attentiveness, and linking them up with other observations and conceptions' (Blendinger).

8

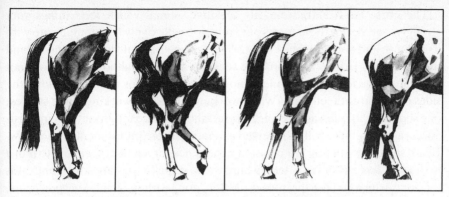

Tail carriage (*from left to right*): normal, excited, active, tensed.

Tail carriage is another form of expression. Enormous efforts are made to get horses to adopt a 'spirited tail carriage', for example, when presenting them to potential buyers. The tail carried to one side is as expressive as a tightly clamped tail, or the stiff, horizontal tail of the excited horse. Horses have far more sensitive reflexes than people, and consequently they react significantly faster than we do. In this respect the heavy coldblood types do not compare with the breedier Arabs and Thoroughbreds.

The peculiarities of the horse's eye will be dealt with in detail in the chapter entitled 'Shying'. But the horse does have two further sensitive and perceptive faculties which must be mentioned here. The first of these is an extraordinarily sensitive skin. The skin in the neck and shoulder zones is particularly sensitive.

Horses love having their withers scratched. Everyone has seen pictures of foals or older horses scratching each other. Scratching a horse's crest is a good way of making friends with it. A horse which will not allow you to catch hold of it by its head can often be persuaded if you run your hand slowly along its crest, from withers to poll, scratching as you go. The part directly above the elbow is less sensitive. The sensitivity of the rib area and flank to the action of the whip or spur varies from one individual to another, and it has not yet been established whether, for example, the many horses which react violently to the whip, and yet have had no bad experience of it, fear it as an invisible enemy. They can, however, be accustomed to it by skilful training.

The sensitivity of the schooled horse to the mere pressure of the leg on the saddle flap is of fundamental importance in dressage training. The contact between horse and rider is established mainly through touch, hearing and smell. The horse has the rider on its back permanently under observation, and still manages to watch what is going on around it at the same time. Since a horse is far more sensitive than its rider, and can concentrate more intensively on him than he on it (provided it is not asked to do so for excessively long periods) it can sense the rider's thoughts, and will react to the slightest suspicion of fear or mistrust, or indeed of happiness and confidence.

The horse's feet offer another example of its sensitivity. The horse is able to pick up the slightest vibrations in the ground through its feet, for example the footsteps of other animals, or man.

We know that wild horses covered long distances every day in search of grazing areas. They alternated between trotting and cantering, with the trot predominating. Hence the manner in which horses are kept nowadays has a profound psychological influence on them. The horse's natural craving for exercise – which reflects its whole lifestyle, and not only the fact that it escapes danger by running – is expressed in the enjoyment it derives from it. This is seen most clearly in horses turned out in the paddock. Horses nowadays, especially sport horses, are usually confined to their stables for twenty-three hours out of twenty-four. Stalls are the worst in this respect, because the horse is tied up all day looking at a blank wall. In many stables, the horses have no contact with the outside world. They have to be at man's beck and call, prepared to do and put up with what man wants, for an hour each day, whether they like it or not. In days gone by, work horses were out and about for many hours each day, so that as well as exercise they had contact with the outside world and with the person who worked them, looked after and fed them. Nowadays, in many cases, the horse is presented to the rider already saddled and bridled, and at the end of the ride it is unsaddled, again probably not by its rider. Most people who keep horses do not realise how much the horse is capable of in terms of performance, and that lack of exercise leads to every conceivable form of mischief and bad behaviour. Lively, intelligent horses in particular tend to react in this way, because they need more exercise and more to occupy them than placid, lethargic animals.

One hour per day of exercise is insufficient, and the pent-up energy seeks an outlet, either in the form of resistance or of a substitute for exercise, and all sorts of almost perverse habits develop. Punishment is not the answer to the problem, which must be solved by means of regular, meaningful work – and more work. It is a proven fact that the horses with the least tendency to develop bad habits are the so-called 'school horses' found in riding establishments, and this is because they are often worked for several hours, carrying and putting up with all sorts of different pupils and their mostly negative influences.

There is a whole range of behaviour problems resulting from the horse resisting excessive demands. Either the trainer has attempted to go too fast, or the goals have been set too high or tackled inexpertly. It is only too easy to sap a horse's enthusiasm for its work (always remember the principle that the horse must be kept in a good mood, i.e. 'sweet'), since excessive demands often lead to painful tendons and joints, and the horse may then have no strength left with

10

which to resist, and will resign itself dejectedly to its fate. Either its spirit is broken (and it may also have suffered irreparable damage to its back and hindquarters because it was asked to do things before it was ready), or it resists with all its remaining strength. It should be a golden rule that the rider or trainer should never resort to coercion until he has exhausted all the other means available and cannot come up with any other solution which is in keeping with the principle of a caring education. This rule was established by De La Guérinière right back in 1733, and there would certainly be fewer broken down, ruined and badly trained horses today if it were respected.

The horse's sexual instincts can also give rise to problems. In recent years, more people have taken to riding stallions, but this does not mean that the problems involved have been overcome. In riding schools and livery yards, stallion keeping is usually fraught with problems. Stallions create unrest in the yard, and it is rarely practical to turn them out. Sometimes they are no trouble at all, but there is as yet no way of ensuring a trouble-free existence with a stallion in the yard. Mares are not troublesome in the same way, but they do have problems of their own at times. The first stage of oestrus or 'heat' is characterised by flirting, enticing and resisting. In the second phase the resistance has disappeared and the mare is ready to be covered. The mare's general behaviour may reflect these tendencies. In the first phase she may be ticklish, she may squeal, make threatening gestures, urinate and swish her tail ('don't touch!'). In the second phase, which often lasts little more than a day, the rider has the impression that he is sitting on a passive, immovable body, over which he has practically no influence, and which is stupified and completely dead to the legs and hands. Not all mares behave in this way, but some do. Mares of this type are unusable to all intents and purposes during these periods. Obviously, punishment is inappropriate. The best thing is to leave them alone.

Perversions (unnatural behaviour) may also arise, in which case the veterinarian should always be called in.

De La Guérinière wrote about 250 years ago: 'One should guard against lumping all the horse's faults together as vices. Usually the horse has simply failed to understand what the rider wants, or else his disobedience is caused by a physical defect'. He adds: 'Aids and punishments should be given discreetly (without unnecessary movement). Their effectiveness lies primarily in the rider's skill and speed of reaction. The punishment must be simultaneous with the fault, otherwise it will do more harm than good. Above all, a horse must never be punished in temper or anger, but always calmly. Finally I should like to say that the ability to use aids and punishments correctly is one of the finest qualities of the horseman'.

Behaviour problems can manifest themselves under saddle or in the stable. Stable vices represent an instinctive attempt to compensate for some deficiency or physical discomfort. The dictionary definition of *Untugenden* (the German word for 'bad habits' or 'vices') is 'behaviour, in domestic animals, which deviates from the normal and habitual behaviour of that species of animal, and which restricts its use or makes it dangerous to associate with. Examples of vices in horses are restiveness, kicking, biting, shying, playing with the tongue, weaving . . .' Then there are also: scratching, masturbating, box walking and extreme timidity.

Horses discover an amazing number of ways to keep themselves busy or to avoid doing something they do not want to do. Apart from the bad habits listed in the dictionary, which may be influenced by heredity, though also by external factors such as incorrect handling, there is a whole range of problems which may affect the horse in the stable, at the blacksmith's, in the field or under saddle. As well as the well-known vices such as biting, kicking and weaving there are many equally unpleasant habits such as rug-tearing, tail rubbing, rubbing the feet together, wind-sucking, crib-biting, pawing the ground, refusing to pick up the feet, tipping feed all over the ground, refusing to leave the stable, pulling back (when tied up), greedy feeding, chewing the edge of the manger, eating dung, eating wood and chewing hair. The latter are signs of deficiencies or metabolic disorders. Abdominal and intestinal disturbances (parasites) can also lead to bad habits. Behaviour problems under saddle are: shying, playing with the tongue, restiveness, refusing to stand while being mounted, blowing the stomach out while being girthed, flapping the lips, gnashing the teeth, catching hold of the bit with the teeth, sticking the tongue out, putting the tongue over the bit, running away, rearing, rubbing the rider against the wall, refusing to go into water, refusing jumps, resisting the spur, lying down (in water), swishing the tail, napping, bucking, shaking the head, tensing under the saddle (cold back) and opening the mouth.

The expression 'restiveness' crops up frequently in old books on riding. The dictionary definition is 'Habitual disobedience and resistance by horse, e.g. misbehaviour in the stable, in harness or at the forge, or out on the roads or in traffic. Restiveness can interfere with, or prevent the use of, the horse in an organised work situation. It may result from inexperience, or it may be inborn or inherited. Physical or psychological disturbances may also be the cause'.

Stable Vices

Wind-sucking and Crib-biting

Wind-sucking and crib-biting are two of the most dreaded vices. They result from boredom, though heredity can also play a part. There is a theory that a horse which is stabled next-door to a crib-biter or wind-sucker will contract the habit itself, which suggests that horses also have an underlying urge to mimic. This urge, combined with curiosity ('What are you up to?'), can certainly lead to a horse adopting the practice.

What is crib-biting? The horse opens its mouth and at the same time contracts the muscles on the underside of the neck. This results in the larynx being locked in position or drawn downwards. The gullet is opened and air can flow into it. This air is then either swallowed or allowed to flow out again, and the dreaded belching noise results. This habit can interfere with the digestive process, sometimes causing severe colic. The incisor teeth are also affected, because in order to contract the necessary muscles, the horse catches hold of something with its teeth, e.g. the edge of the manger, or even the top of its own fore leg.

In wind-sucking, as opposed to crib-biting, the horse manages to contract the necessary muscles to suck in the air without catching hold of anything in its teeth.

In Germany, crib-biting and wind-sucking are vices which must, by law, be declared when a horse is offered for sale. Although every horse owner must be wary of horses with these vices, many such horses suffer no adverse effects, i.e. they have no feeding problems and are not prone to colic as a result of this practice. This behaviour problem can also arise as a result of feeding the wrong things, such as sugar in particular. Any observant horseman will have noticed that after a horse has been eating sugar it starts licking its manger, the walls of the stable etc. Although it still has a long way to go – from licking to nibbling, then biting, then clamping its jaw, and then finally sucking air – this is where it all starts. One often hears that horses should not be fed titbits, let alone sugar, in the stable, and this is why. These habits can also develop as a result of an attempt by the horse to alleviate an empty feeling in its stomach, for example, when it has been fed too much concentrate and insufficient bulk food. All too often there is a tendency to give the horse too little exercise and at the same time to feed it up with too much concentrate and cut down on the roughage. When the unfortunate animal then attempts to make up for this by eating its own bed, it is put on sawdust or peat and does not see any long feed the whole day through. However, it is also possible to feed too much bulk feed; the normal ration is from 4.5 to 6.8 kg of hay and from 2.3 to 3.6 kg of straw. It is a good idea to split the overall daily ration into six to eight small feeds in order to keep the horse occupied. As well as having a nutritional value, bulk food also serves to prevent the horse getting bored, especially at night. The largest portion of bulk food should be fed in the evening. Giving the horse sufficient bulk feed prevents it getting into bad habits out of boredom.

Projections, bars and protruding edges also provide the horse with an opportunity to adopt bad habits in that it will tend to catch hold of them or chew them out of boredom or to amuse itself. The edges of mangers should be wide enough for the horse not to be able to catch hold of them. Concrete and porcelain mangers tend to be thick enough already by way of their construction. Some plastic mangers have replaceable edges because the manufacturers realise that this part is the most vulnerable. Some horses attack the edges of their mangers with relish. Giving the horse something to play with in the stable is one solution. This subject will be dealt with in more detail in the chapter on 'Chewing'. The stable should be a place where the horse can rest, but not where its mind becomes stultified.

It is, therefore, very important that horses with a tendency to crib-bite should be given the least possible opportunity to do so. When designing stables for such horses the above must be taken into account, and in existing stables all projections, bars etc., which could fit into a horse's mouth should be removed. It makes no sense to have dividing walls made of vertical wooden bars wide enough apart for the horse to get its mouth round them, or horizontal rails which are ideal for chewing, or nailed planks just right for pulling off and eating. A stable wall should be smooth. If a see-through partition is required, heavy-gauge wire-mesh in a steel frame is a practical solution, with the holes too small for the horse to get its teeth through. The best way to feed hay is off the ground. Oats and concentrates should also be fed off the ground in a sieve or bowl which can be removed afterwards. Though the food sometimes gets dirty, this is the most natural way for the horse to eat. Mangers fitted to the rear wall of the box have sometimes proven successful, because horses usually stand at the front of the box and if they are going to get up to mischief they tend to do so there. The disadvantage is that you have to go inside the box to feed the horse, but it must surely be worth the inconvenience if it solves the problem.

What should you do if your horse crib-bites or wind-sucks, or is starting to do so? It is noticeable that lively horses are particularly prone to this habit. When, through too much standing around doing nothing, the horse has contracted this habit, it will not give it up unless something is done to prevent it. The horse can become so 'practised' in the art that it no longer needs to catch hold of anything

Crib-biting horse and resulting damage to the teeth. Similar damage occurs to the teeth of horses which grind them (on bars, etc.). Painting the paddock fence with preparations of various kinds has little effect.

in its teeth to wind-suck. In this case it is no use just removing everything the horse can grasp. A wind-sucking strap can help up to a point though it must be worn all the time except when the horse is working. It can be used on both crib-biters and wind-suckers, though it is a prevention and not a cure. It must fit properly and not be too loose, or too tight. It is attached to the headcollar by a strap at the poll to prevent it slipping down the neck.

This strap is a half-measure which has its disadvantages. The horse will try to rub it off, and if it is not tight enough the horse soon learns how to wind-suck in spite of it, even if not to the same extent. Horses still in the early stages of the habit can sometimes be cured by means of a 'flute' bit (wind-sucking bit) attached to the headcollar. Like the wind-sucking strap it must be worn all the time, both in the stable and in the field. A Tattersall ring bit achieves the same result by stopping the horse wanting to play with things with its mouth. However these measures must be used immediately, before the habit becomes ingrained.

Electrified wire has proven fairly successful for deterring crib-biters from catching hold of paddock fencing. The electrical pulse in the wire is so un-pleasant for the horse that at least it respects the rails in its paddock. The same method can even be used in the stable if there are projections on the inside

Wind-sucking strap, Tattersall ring bit and flute bit (with keys).

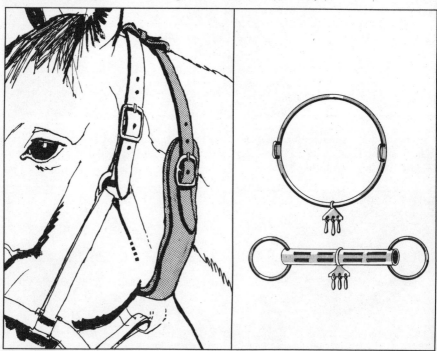

walls. In fact you must use any means you can to outwit your horse, who will, in his turn, find the most devious ways to indulge his habit.

A further course of action is surgery, in which the sternal, oesophageal and submaxillary muscles involved in wind-sucking and crib-biting are cut on the underside of the neck near the throat. This is a drastic, expensive and messy operation, which leaves a visible break in the musculature which makes up the bottom line of the neck. This break varies in size depending on the skill of the surgeon. About 80 per cent of horses operated upon in this way are permanently cured of their habit. In my experience, once the decision has been made to take action against an established crib-biter, this is the best solution. The scar left by the operation grows together perfectly, leaving only a slight disturbance of the lower line of the neck. The less developed the underside of the neck, and the greater the surgeon's skill in making a, so to speak, cosmetically balanced cut in the musculature, the less significant will this disturbance of the neckline be. You need a strong stomach to be able to watch this operation.

Painting surfaces with tar or other coatings is only successful up to a point. Apart from the fact that the horses get covered in them, they do not last, and it does not always solve the problem.

Chewing

Horses may chew, or lick, the walls of their stables from boredom or for amusement or because they are suffering from a salt or mineral deficiency. Eating soil or dung is also caused by a deficiency. In days gone by, horses used to eat grasses and herbs in a set order, and so kept themselves 'topped up' with the minerals they needed. Nowadays horses are cooped up in their boxes for far too long each day and are fed on specified foods year in, year out. They cannot look for what they need, but instead have to eat what is put in front of them. M. Schäfer says that for this reason, when feeding in the winter, he adheres as closely as possible to the horse's natural choice of plants by feeding the best, sweet hay in the morning, and sweet hay plus hay from acid meadows in the evening. The horse's roughage requirement must be satisfied, even in cases where the crude fibre intake has to be rationed to prevent the horse getting too fat. Often horses are bedded on peat or sawdust because they have attempted to compensate for the shortage of bulk food by eating straw bedding, even when it is dirty. Schäfer speaks of 'feeding factors', which are requirements that need to be satisfied. Normally a horse spends a total of twelve hours a day eating. If this requirement is not fulfilled there is a risk that the desire to eat will lead, for example, to the horse chewing anything it can get hold of, the more so because its ancestors obtained essential substances by chewing bark and branches.

The best way to satisfy the requirement for salt is to hang a salt-lick in the stable. This is better than adding a few spoonfuls of salt to the feed. It is also a good idea to put branches in the stable for the horse to chew, if for no other reason than to keep it occupied. Obviously the branches must not come from acacia, yew, conifer or box trees since they are poisonous to horses. Bark contains tannin, the exact amount depends on the type of tree, and branches with buds on them contain bitter substances which horses will eat. Young horses in particular, being more active than older ones, enjoy having a branch or twig to occupy themselves with, though it should not be too thin. An empty cardboard box – without metal staples in it, of course – can also be put in the stable. A horse with a lively mind will find all sorts of things to do with it!

'Mane chewing' is associated with back and wither scratching. Two horses scratching each other's backs from crest to tail with their teeth make a charming sight, but the result in terms of damage to the mane is catastrophic. Before

Branch placed in the stable for the horse to chew.

long, unsightly holes appear in the beautifully tended mane, and it is weeks or months before the chewed tufts of hair have grown back again. In short, the mane looks thoroughly moth-eaten. To put it just as bluntly, there is nothing that can be done about it. It cannot be termed a bad habit since nibbling the mane is part of normal social grooming, in which horses (provided they are friends) will nibble each other in the places they cannot reach on themselves. This is an occupation to which horses are completely devoted, and it is out of the question to try to stop it. The only thing you can do is split up the two horses concerned into different paddocks, because, as has already been said: when it comes to getting your back scratched, not just anyone will do!

Grinding the teeth on the bars

Deformed incisor teeth are also the sign of the advanced stage of another bad habit: grinding the teeth on the bars. In order to understand this habit we must first make a brief study of the horse's eating habits. Horses living in the wild used to eat over the course of the whole day. The size of the horse's stomach does not permit it to take in a large quantity of food all at once, like cattle do. Except when it is desperately hungry, the horse bites off a few blades of grass at a time, chews them thoroughly and swallows them. Consequently, to get enough food, it has to eat for at least five hours. In contrast, horses nowadays are fed at specified times. Since it is known that a horse cannot make do with one meal per day, as a dog can, it is fed three times per day. Feed times should be strictly adhered to.

The horse has a strong sense of time. For example, school horses know exactly when the lesson time is 'up'. There are numerous stories about carters and grooms and their horses which demonstrate the horse's awareness of time. Interestingly, the horse's inner clock is always slightly 'fast', making the horse react before the time arrives for something to happen. Unrest automatically sets in in the stables as the normal feed-time approaches. It is therefore essential to keep exactly to these feed times in order to avoid further confusion. Horses quickly get into bad habits as a means of working off their feelings, and these habits are further exacerbated by the desire for food.

Obsession with food is less pronounced in herds of horses grazing on large areas of grassland. The horses keep their distances, and only graze close together if they are especially close friends. In stables the situation is very different. The increased preoccupation with food is (according to Blendinger) a manifestly neurotic exaggeration of a primitive natural mode of behaviour. Obvious signs are laid-back ears, bared teeth, kicking the sides of the stable, grinding the teeth on the partition bars etc. Here again it is the energetic, intelligent horses which express themselves most forcefully.

Grinding the teeth along the bars of the partition grille or on the edge of the manger has particularly unpleasant consequences if the latter are made of metal. Before long, blemishes and signs of abnormal wear appear on the incisor teeth, and the horse's ability to eat (graze) may be impaired. Here again, the first course of action is to remove all opportunities for practising the habit. This is easier said than done, but as a horse-keeper one should go to the trouble to

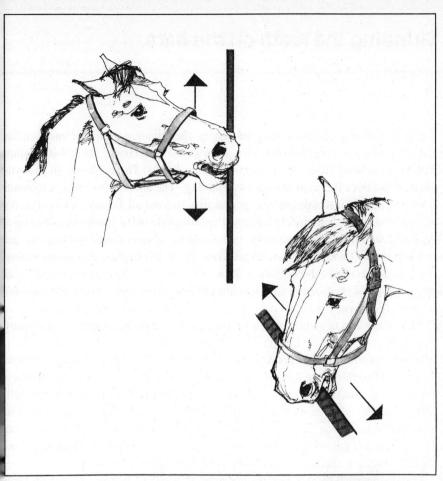

Grinding the teeth on vertical bars and horizontal objects is particularly harmful when these are made of metal, because they act like a rasp. Concrete is no better.

ensure that there is as little as possible for the horse to catch hold of in its teeth. It is also a good idea either to feed such horses before the others, or to tie them up temporarily in such a way that they cannot get hold of anything.

Banging and kicking the sides of the stable

The causes of this habit are the same as the previous one. Again, the horses concerned are not of a dull, indolent nature, they are lively, active and sensitive. They kick the sides of the stable out of excitement and impatience, and also to draw attention to themselves. Moreover, man is partly to blame for this habit: the bad practice of distributing titbits encourages horses to beg, and to try to get attention by pawing or banging. Not only is this an annoying habit, but knocking the limbs against the walls can have unpleasant consequences, such as capped hocks. If not treated immediately these can become hard and press on the joint, with even more unpleasant results. The knees too can be damaged. Remedial measures consist on the one hand in padding the sides of the box, and on the other in strict adherence to the rule that the horses must not be encouraged to beg. If the kicking results from a preoccupation with food, tying the horse up at feed times should be considered.

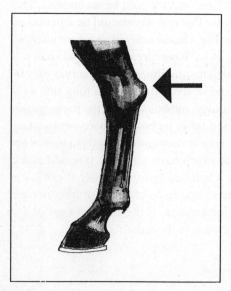

Capped hock.

24

Pawing

Pawing the ground in the stable is always a sign of impatience and a craving for exercise; a tired horse rarely paws, except when it intends to lie down. With this as with the other habits, it makes absolutely no sense to shout at the horse and punish it with a whip in an attempt to stop it. This sort of treatment will only lead to restlessness, head-shyness and resistance, in fact quite the opposite of the desired result. Here again the principle applies that disobedient horses are only made obedient through work. As well as taking pleasure in exercise, the horse has a physical craving for it. When it paws the ground, this means that it wants something – or at least it wants something other than to stand in its stable. Pawing is a way of expressing eagerness and impatience; it is the horse's way of saying 'I want'. If the horse has discovered that it obtains something from man when it paws, it will quickly get into the habit of begging, and then you will never stop it from doing it. Horses also paw when they are hungry or thirsty, without the handler having done anything to cause it. Here again they are trying to say that they want to go out – to get a drink or something to eat.

Pawing can also mean, of course, that the horse is ill. The accompanying symptoms are well known, and this is not the place to discuss them.

In this connection the weekly 'day off' (rest day) should be mentioned. The latter is an example of misplaced kindness. The rest day should be a period of relaxation, not time spent doing nothing. For a horse a day of enforced idleness is not a rest day but sheer torment and, as we have already seen and shall see again, it causes numerous behaviour problems and illnesses, and serves only to keep the vets in business. The worst kind of day off follows a long ride or a competition. The ride takes place on a Sunday, for example, so the horse spends half of Sunday plus all of Monday cooped up in its box, perhaps with aching muscles, and is thus deprived of the exercise it desperately needs to loosen up its muscles and work off the lactic acids which have built up. It would make more sense to put a headcollar on one's beloved horse and take it out for a walk. A rest from being ridden and from stress, and a measure of freedom are what is required. If this is impossible, for example if the horse is kept in the middle of a town, it should at least be let loose in the indoor school for a while.

Throwing feed about

Some horses toss their food right and left over the sides of the manger onto the floor before they actually start eating. This is a senseless trick, since they then proceed to pick it all up again out of the straw. Foals often pick up this habit from their dams. The first course of action is to put only part of the feed in the manger at a time: a full manger only serves to encourage this sort of behaviour. If there is only enough food to cover the bottom of the manger this will cramp the horse's style! A second possibility is to change the manger. You can now buy mangers with an inner lip which prevents the food being pushed out. You can also fit bars across the manger. This will stop the horse swinging its head from side to side and so knocking the food out. A manger with a large lump in the bottom will also make it difficult for the horse to push the food out, because it will have to put its nose down by the sides of the lump to reach it. If the manger is big enough, a salt lick, whole or in pieces, can be put in the bottom.

Another solution worth considering is to feed the horse on the ground, either out of a shallow trough which can be removed afterwards, or, if the ground surface is suitable and clean, directly off the ground. There is no reason why the horse should not eat off the ground as nature intended. The only prerequisite, as has already been said, is an area of clean floor from which it can eat its feed without picking up pieces of dirt, sand and wood.

Some horses are masters of the art of dismantling and destroying any manger, especially the plastic kind, in record time. They should either be given a concrete manger, or should be fed on the ground. This will also prevent the damage sometimes caused to the fore legs, e.g. the knees by demolishing feed containers placed on the ground.

Weaving

Weaving is a tiresome habit in which the stationary horse rocks its forehand continuously from side to side, usually with its fore legs slightly apart. The weight is transferred from one fore leg to the other, which causes undue wear and tear on the joints and tendons of the fore legs, the more so since this swinging may go on for hours on end. Weaving is without a doubt a way of compensating for lack of exercise. Other animals kept in captivity (e.g. elephants, camels and bears), are also prone to weaving. It can spread from one horse to another, so, bearing in mind that horses like to imitate, weavers should be placed where other horses cannot see them.

In well designed yards, the stable doors open outwards over the yard. The

In weaving, the tendons, ligaments and joints of the fore legs are continuously under stress.

top part of the doors can be left open. The horses can watch what is going on in the yard, can see each other, get plenty of fresh air, and do not feel hemmed in – or at least we think they do not. In fact we are wrong, since horses stabled in this way often weave. It is true that they can feel part of what is going on, but they cannot go out of their boxes, however comfortable these may be, and they may then begin to weave as a way of compensating for this. Matters are made worse if there is something exciting going on outside the stable, either to one side or, worse still, directly opposite. It is advisable to keep the top door shut and to open the bottom one.

Rocking from side to side with excitement when the feed is due can also lead to weaving. As has already been said, horses know exactly when it is feed time.

Once a horse has started to weave, it is extremely difficult, if not impossible, to stop it. Weights attached to the fetlocks have been tried, but here the risk of injury has to be taken into account. As with all bad habits, you have to experiment with the unlikeliest of cures in order to find one which works. People have tried painting black and white vertical stripes on the walls of the stable so the horse has the impression, when it weaves, that the stripes are oscillating. Attaching weights to the body which make counter movements when the horse weaves have also been found helpful. Another method is to attach to the headcollar a rope with a weight on the end. The rope goes through a ring on the wall, and whenever the horse weaves it has to pull the weight; this can be a stone weighing about 11 kg. It is quite possible that weaving then becomes simply too much bother! Horses which receive sufficient exercise, either in the form of work or through being turned out, rarely take up weaving.

A habit not far removed from weaving is eternally walking round in circles in the box. As a basic principle, a tired horse will rarely show any desire to box-walk. Horses adopt this practice through boredom. A stable companion, in the form of a goat, for example, should be considered. There are many cases of friendships between animals, with both animals benefiting from the relationship.

Treading on the opposite foot, and crossing the feet

With the first habit the horse treads on, or rubs, the coronet of one hind foot with the opposite foot. This often results in injury to the coronet. Like the previous habit, this is difficult to cure and results from boredom. The only possible course of action is to fit over-reach boots, so that at least the horse cannot injure itself.

With the second habit the horse stands with one fore foot crossed over the other. Here again, over-reach boots offer the best protection against injury.

In winter, particular attention should be paid to the removal of all studs for the period that the horse is in the stable. It has become general practice now to leave them in, but the effort should be made, since these are an additional source of injury (e.g. abscesses).

Crossing the feet.

Treading on the coronet of the opposite foot.

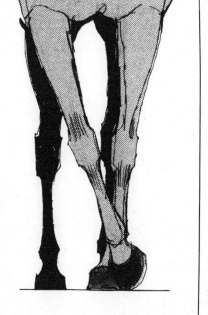

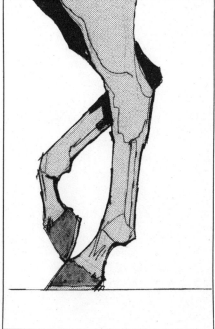

Rubber over-reach boots: pull-on and quick-release.

It is also advisable to consult the veterinary surgeon if there is any suspicion that the horse is resting one foot on the other to take the strain off its tendons. If this is the case the horse is probably suffering from inflammation of the suspensory ligament.

Rubbing the tail

This problem is more common in summer than in winter: the horse has an itch so it rubs the top of its tail on walls, railings or trees. First the hairs become dishevelled, then a bald patch appears, and, in advanced cases, sores develop. The itch is either on the dock, or in the anus or genital region. In the first case dirt is the cause. The hairs at the top of the tail should therefore be brushed meticulously every day with a dandy brush. Sweating horses in particular provide a favourable habitat for the mange mite, and if mange is the cause of the horse rubbing its tail, the veterinary surgeon must be informed because this

Rubbing the tail, and the consequences.

is a notifiable disease. In both the above cases a 2 per cent solution of salicylic acid (salicylic acid collodion) or a 10 per cent solution of benzyl benzoate (in alcohol) has been shown to be effective. When working with this solution, care should be taken that it does not come in contact with the anal or genital area. It goes without saying that the anus and underside of the dock should be washed daily with a sponge.

The itching may also be caused by worms. The veterinary surgeon will advise on this. Horses should, in any case, be wormed several times a year. Grass proteins or allergies to weeds can also cause itching. Here again the veterinary surgeon must be called in.

Mares in season also tend to rub their tails. Using a tail guard or bandaging the tail is helpful in this case.

Tail guard and bandaged tail.

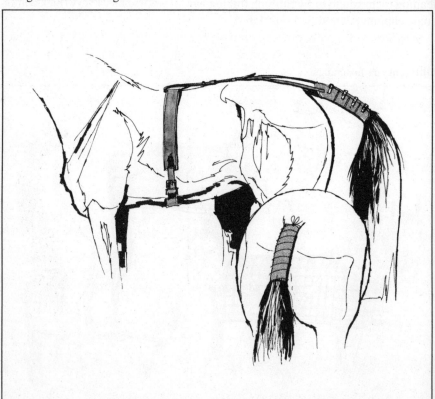

Rug-tearing

Rug-tearing is an expensive habit. Rugs are not cheap, and some horses will reduce any rug to shreds. Unless the cause of this practice is skin irritation, it simply means that the horse does not wish to wear a rug on its back. Horses are rugged much too often, and, on occasions, when rugging is not appropriate. The horse's protective covering, that is, the coat, is designed in such a way that the stabled horse can withstand temperatures as low as −6°C. The important thing is that there are no draughts and that the atmosphere is not damp or steamy. Horses will not come to any harm from dry, cool or cold air provided they are properly fed and have a good bed. So why rug at all? Sweating horses should never be put away until they have been thoroughly dried out, either by leading them round or by rubbing them down. If a horse has a very thick winter coat, clipping should be considered.

Sick horses do, however, sometimes need to be rugged. So what should be

Different rug fastenings.

done if the horse is still in sufficiently good spirits to try to get rid of its rug? Often the rug is not quite straight, it slips under the horse's tummy during the night, and the horse tries to rid itself of its uncomfortable burden. It can also happen that the rug gets torn as the horse stands up, because the horse has trodden on it or become entangled in it. It then hangs down round its legs. The horse may also panic if the rug slips off over its head or is left dangling around its neck and over its head. Rugs should fit in such a way that they cannot slip. In addition to a crupper they should have a sewn-on surcingle which fastens round the belly. Obviously, they must also have a breast strap at the front. Diagonal straps at the back, holding the rear ends of the rug together under the horse's belly, are also a good idea. A second surcingle about 20 cm behind the first is recommended. This helps hold the rug in position and makes it more secure. The above methods of attachment ensure, once and for all, that the rug does not become a nuisance by slipping.

A proven device for preventing rug-tearing is a muzzle or mouth guard. It does not look very nice, and it verges on cruelty because it prevents the horse from eating and drinking. The horse – especially if it has a lively temperament – will try everything to get the muzzle off or to demolish it. A chain muzzle is better because it allows the horse to eat and drink to some extent, but prevents it from getting hold of the rug in its teeth.

Different types of muzzle.

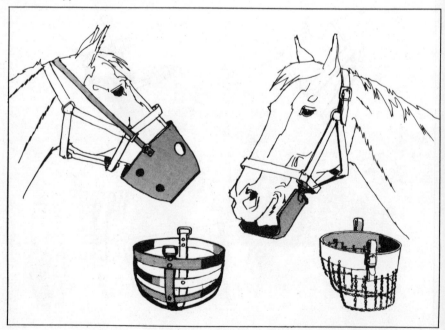

Another possibility is a clothing bib, which is like the back half of a muzzle. This also allows the horse to eat – but not bite its rug. This device is particularly recommended.

Two further pieces of equipment should be mentioned, though they are not recommended. The first is a wooden collar made of slats, which is known as a neck cradle. The horse is able to eat and to move its head, but it cannot turn its head, and so cannot reach its rug. This device is unpleasantly restrictive. Even worse is an anti-rug-tearing bar, which is attached at one end to the headcollar and at the other end to the roller. This is even more restrictive than the cradle. It allows hardly any movement at all and is definitely cruel. Even tying the horse up for long periods is more humane than these two methods.

Devices used for preventing rug tearing: *left*: neck cradle; *below*: bar; *right*: clothing bib.

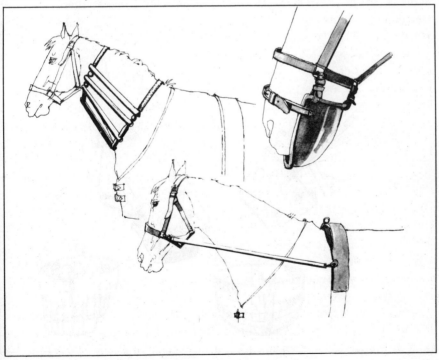

Biting

Biting has various causes. It may result from teasing, desire for food, or incorrect grooming. It may also be a symptom of lack of exercise. Often it has developed, through incorrect education, when the horse was a foal. Young foals entice people into playing with them, especially if there are no other foals in the field, and before long the games become rather rough. The foal does not realise how strong it is in comparison to man; it looks upon him first as a playmate and then as a sparring partner, and soon loses its respect for man.

The human partner may then react by making rapid threatening movements, and by hitting the horse. The horse's confidence is shaken and it reacts by retaliation, e.g. by biting. Quick and energetic action is then necessary to nip this habit in the bud.

Ticklish horses soon restort to biting if subjected to rough treatment while grooming, therefore soft brushes and gentle grooming strokes should be used on the horse's sensitive areas. Horses, and mares in particular, often bite when the saddle is being put on or the girth is being done up. They sink their teeth into the manger or a post, or into the person who is causing the discomfort. Particularly sensitive and strong-willed horses are prone to this habit. In such cases the handler should consider how he can make the unpleasant procedure more acceptable to the horse. Hitting the horse is pointless, as is shouting at it. Talking softly and fondly is a better course of action. Diverting the horse's attention should also be tried. The girth should be done up very loosely, and perhaps only on one strap. Sometimes it also helps to lead the horse forward a few steps, then tighten the girth a bit more. The rider should be helped on, then the saddle is not pulled out of position, and the horse does not feel restricted by a tight girth. It is better to give the horse a titbit as a reward or diversion, or to pat it on the neck, than to abuse it, which it does not understand and which does not prevent it feeling the girth tightening round it.

Horses often become vicious through incorrect handling; in days gone by they were even taught to bite and kick in battle. Modern selective breeding procedures serve to eliminate negative characteristics, so that nowadays horses are rarely born vicious.

An energetic 'lead mare' turned out with horses at grass will usually ensure that order is maintained. A pecking order is quickly established, with a minimum of biting! When man intrudes in this society matters take a different course. Jealousy, aggression and ill-will can turn horses into biters. However, there are many cases of biters turning into pleasant, useful animals once their confidence has been restored. Often, swapping stables or transferring the horse to another block or yard will bring about a change, because behaviour in the stable also depends on the horse's attitude to its neighbours. Horses have strong likes and dislikes. If horses are unsettled, neuroses often develop.

A person whom the horse accepts should be chosen for the job of reforming a biter. A horse's attitude to people also varies. It is wrong to isolate biters. Care should be taken to ensure that they are not teased in the stable. It is a good idea, when trying to cure them, to let them go a bit hungry, so that their interest is focused on the food and not on their human handler. Here also, talking soothingly to the horse is beneficial.

Máday says that, according to the experience of a certain circus director, it is possible to break the horse of this habit by teaching it to retrieve objects. Another view is that it is best to get rid of a chronic biter at the earliest opportunity.

Kicking, and difficulties with shoeing

Another form of malicious behaviour is kicking. However, like biters, kickers are not born that way, even though young foals make reflex movements with their hind legs which can hardly result from experience. Horses become kickers through incorrect handling. The reaction to wrong handling can reach the point where the horse lays back its ears and lashes out at the very approach of a person. Some horses are masters of the art of suddenly lashing out without any visible warning signs. However, a clear distinction must be made between kicking out of malice and kicking because the horse is over-fresh, anxious to be fed, in oestrus, pregnant or ticklish. There is a saying 'Beware of the front legs of a stallion and the hind legs of a mare'. Another saying, which refers to kicking at feeding time, is 'If you want to discover a person's true character, disturb him when he is asleep; if you want to discover a horse's true nature, all you need do is disturb it at feed-time'.

We shall deal first with the habit of lashing out at people. Kicking under saddle will be discussed separately. Kickers are more difficult to deal with in stalls than in loose boxes. Never approach a kicker from behind! Talk to it first, then walk briskly up to it without hesitating. Once the horse has succeeded in frightening its rider or handler, it will always have the upper hand. In most cases of kicking, mistakes have been made when the horse was a foal.

Foals should be accustomed at an early age to having their feet picked up, being handled all over, and being groomed. A little trouble at the outset pays dividends in later years. However, the training must be serious and purposeful, and the foal must not look upon it as a game. Teasing and exciting the foal are fatal. It is also essential that the foal knows its place; a well-timed stroke of the whip will often suffice to make an aggressive horse see sense.

Kicking among horses turned out at grass can only be prevented, and not cured. The first essential is to remove the hind shoes of the kicker. The risk of injury is too great with shoes on. Unless you can spare the time to stand on guard with a whip for hours on end, kickers should be turned out separately. It is also advisable to round off the corners of the field with diagonal rails to prevent a horse being trapped in a corner in case of an argument.

In days gone by, kickers were hobbled in the stable, or had ropes attached to their hind feet at one end and to their headcollars at the other, and run through a ring attached to the lower part of the roller. The result was that the horse

Rounding off the corners of the paddock with diagonal rails prevents horses from being trapped in the corner and kicked.

punished itself when it kicked. Turning the horse round temporarily in its stall can be helpful, and at least it allows the stable work to be done in safety. However the best solution is to try to win back the horse's confidence with endless patience and calmness. Here again the horse's liking for its groom or rider plays an important part, and the horse should be attended in its stable by this person only.

As with pawing, striking out with the front feet is caused by impatience (unless it is an expression of pain, e.g. colic). There is one quite aggressive form of this habit, which has usually developed from 'begging'. Of course you must give your horse treats, but horses differ in their natures, and we must know where to draw the line if the 'begging' starts to get out of hand. If your horse does start striking out with its fore feet at people, the whip is the only answer. However, its use (from the front, on the cannon bone) must be spontaneous and immediate. If you have to run and fetch the whip the punishment is too late, and is ineffectual, because the horse cannot associate the two events.

Particular calmness and firmness are necessary when it comes to shoeing. Here again the first mistakes are often made during the foal's early education. A foal's feet must be carefully trimmed to prevent incurable position faults in later years. The young horse must therefore learn to have its feet picked up. Now and then it will be necessary to hang on tight, because once the horse has learned that the handler is not so strong as itself, it will keep on trying to pull its foot away.

Often, however, people go about picking the feet up wrongly. The horse will lift both fore and hind legs more easily if they are pulled forward slightly. Bending the fore leg at the knee can also be tried. The leg is held by the fetlock,

 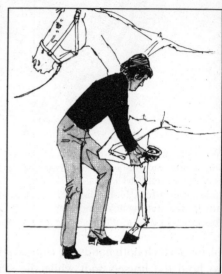

Lifting up a fore foot. To make it easier to hold the foot up, it is advisable to rest the horse's knee on your thigh.

Lifting up a hind foot. The foot can be rested on your thigh.

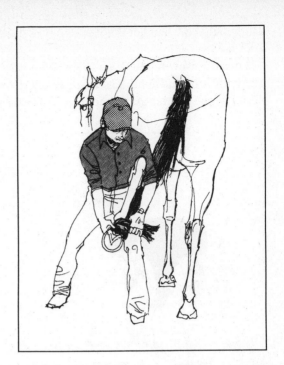

Winding the end of the horse's tail around the hind foot while it is in the air tends to have a quietening effect. It also has the advantage that the horse more or less holds its own foot up.

around which both hands are cupped. (On the Continent a helper is employed to hold the horse's foot while the smith shoes it.) With the hind leg it is important that the fetlock rests on the handler's thigh so that it cannot be pulled away. It is a good idea for a helper to distract the horse's attention by playing with its top lip or stroking its forehead. An easy way to hold up the hind foot is to wrap the horse's tail around the fetlock. Then if it kicks out it punishes itself by wrenching its tail.

If a horse refuses to lift up its feet, or manages to kick while it is being shod, and all attempts to distract its attention have failed, then a sedative in the feed, or an injection from the vet, or the twitch, are the only answer. It must be remembered when using a twitch that the purpose of this device is to distract the horse and not to inflict pain. In other words it should not be twisted so tight that the end of the nose turns blue or the skin comes off. The twitch should be used to play with the end of the horse's nose, and should only be turned more tightly when necessary. It should be loosened as soon as the horse does what is required of it. Patting the horse lightly on the neck and speaking soothingly to it at the same time help it to calm down and not think about what is happening to its feet.

It is also a good idea to tire the horse by riding it before it is due to be shod. It cannot be stressed too much that most bad behaviour would never arise in the first place if horses were worked sufficiently, and, above all, regularly.

The twitch should never be kept permanently tight: it should be loosened when the horse has done what is required. The, unfortunately, common practice of tying the twitch in position (*right*) is totally unacceptable.

Kicking the sides of the box or the stall partitions can have unpleasant consequences. Bruises and capped hocks are common occurrences in such cases. One way of reducing the damage is to pad the walls. Swinging bail partitions in stalls should have plaited straw wrapped round them. Particularly in the primitive stabling provided at competitions, care must be taken that kickers cannot do any damage, the more so since competition horses wear studs in their hind shoes. Also, the bails are often attached only at the front end, and the rear end lies on the ground.

To cure a kicker in days gone by, a leather strap was put round the horse's leg above the hock. To this was attached an iron ball, or a stone, on a string. The weight hung level with the cannon bone and struck the horse if it kicked.

Everyone has seen the red ribbon on the tail of some ridden horses out hunting or hacking. This indicates a potential kicker, and means one should take care and keep one's distance. Finally it must be mentioned that kicking the wall may be a sign that something is wrong, for example irritation caused by sallenders, or an injury, may be the cause, or the horse may be suffering from abdominal pains. In such cases the veterinary surgeon must be consulted.

Refusing to be shod is a very common example of bad behaviour. Once again, the roots of this problem are usually to be found in the handling of the horse as a foal. Allowing its feet to be picked up is something a horse learns relatively easily, but all too often young horses are allowed to get away with stroppy behaviour, and handling the feet may even be omitted altogether (to the detriment of the posture of the legs and feet), or be carried out in a rough

42

and ready fashion, which, in its turn, causes the young horse to react. A tried and tested method of making foals behave, and making it easier for the blacksmith to trim the feet, is the following: a suitable stable is chosen, and plenty of straw is put down so that the foal cannot slip. A helper leads the foal up to the wall and stays with it throughout the operation, talking to it soothingly, patting it and praising it. A second helper pushes the foal's croup up against the wall, lifting up the tail as he does so. The blacksmith can then see to the foal's feet by himself. Good handling, sensitivity, time and patience make strong treatment mostly unnecessary.

The blacksmith's work is hard enough, without him having to cope with a horse which will not stand but hops around on three legs. We have already discussed picking up the feet, the use of the twitch to distract the horse where necessary, and of sedative injections given by the vet. In days gone by, when it was the horses which went to the blacksmith, and not the blacksmith who came

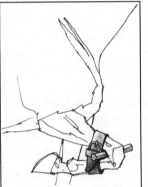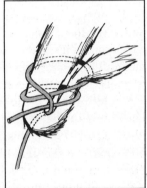

(*Left*): Raising and securing the fore leg and the hind leg of a kicker. In an emergency the stick (which must be round) can be pulled out quickly.

(*Right*): The correct way to secure a tail.

A good method, though it can present problems (e.g. how to get the strap round the pastern).

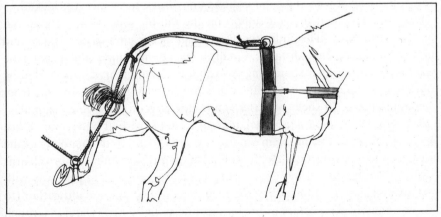

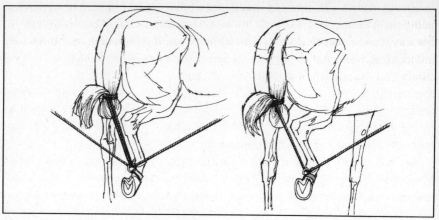

Two more ways of holding up the hind foot of a kicker: *left:* method for use with two helpers; *right:* method for use with one helper.

to the horses, the unfamiliar surroundings paralysed the horses with tension and made them more biddable. The blacksmiths also had a 'shoeing frame', which immobilised the horse completely. To complete the picture, two more methods of making recalcitrant horses lift their hind feet can be adopted, both of which rely on the use of a rope.

Similar problems can arise when the veterinary surgeon calls. Some vets know how to deal with difficult horses, and others do not. Horses are very easily put off. One clumsily given injection is enough. Next time the horse flies into a panic at the sight of the vet at the stable door. The only way round the problem is great tact, practise – or another vet.

Nervous horses sometimes react by trying to crush their groom, or anyone else for that matter, against the wall, an unpleasant and seemingly threatening practice. Usually it is a sign of terror, and not of malice. A horse trying to avoid being kicked by another horse can be seen to protect itself by leaning its flank against the flank of the other horse. Hence when a horse crushes a person against a wall because it is afraid of punishment, this is a defensive reaction and not a malicious one. This must be understood, and the horse not be punished for it. It makes more sense to calm the horse and convince it that there is nothing to be afraid of.

Finally a few words about kicking from over-freshness. Many an accident has been caused by horses being led and released incorrectly, for example, when they are turned out in the field. Horses should be obedient, and they can be trained to go quietly and obediently to the field. Taking two horses to the field at the same time should be avoided wherever possible. Too many things can go wrong on the way to the field and when entering it. It is a big mistake to release the horse at the gate and let it go charging off. This is where kicking can have disastrous effects. On entering the field the horse should be turned so that it is facing the handler, and it should not be released until it is standing quietly. In this way it can never reach him with its feet even if it then charges off bucking and kicking. Believe it or not, it is quite possible to educate a horse to behave calmly and quietly when it is given its freedom.

Getting cast

Getting cast is not a vice. However, some horses manage to get cast time and time again even in large stables, which means that it can still be termed a bad habit, though one which is caused by clumsiness. Horses can also get cast in stalls. Obviously the first thing to do when this happens is to release the horse from the tie rope or chain; if this cannot be done, the headcollar must be cut off. In stalls partitioned with swinging bails the rest is simple: the bail is detached, the adjacent horse moved out, and the horse is able to get up by itself. With solid partitions or loose boxes (the normal size for a full-sized horse is 3 by 3.5 m), help must be summoned and attempts made to move the horse into a better position by pulling it round by its tail or by ropes attached to its feet. This should be done calmly so as not to panic the horse. Care must be exercised when pulling the horse by the tail – a broken tail is a nasty injury! It is a mistake to hit the horse to try to make it get up when it is simply not in a position to do so. As a last resort, ropes and slings can be used.

Obviously the above advice refers to healthy horses which cannot get up because they are stuck. Horses which cannot get up through illness should, of course, be referred to the vet. A horse gets up in the opposite sequence to a cow. It rolls onto its tummy and brings its hind legs as far forward as possible under its body. It then extends its fore legs one at a time to the front and uses them to lift the body. This enables the hind legs to push off from the ground with a jolt, which goes right through the body. This sequence must be understood because this knowledge will enable the handler to put the horse's legs in a position which will make it easier for it to get up.

When attaching slings to help the horse up, care must be taken to prevent it becoming excited. If it does panic it is advisable (to prevent the horse wasting its energy as well as to stop it being injured) to pin its head to the ground by getting an assistant to kneel on its neck and press down with his hands on the jaw bone or behind the ears. Many horses will take over as soon as they feel the ground under their feet, but some, either through shock or extreme weakness, have to be pulled all the way up into a standing position, and even then it is a while before they actually take their weight on their feet. Here again the veterinary surgeon should be consulted.

Horses which find difficulty in standing up should be provided with a deep litter straw bed, or a bed with a layer of peat underneath. This enables the horse

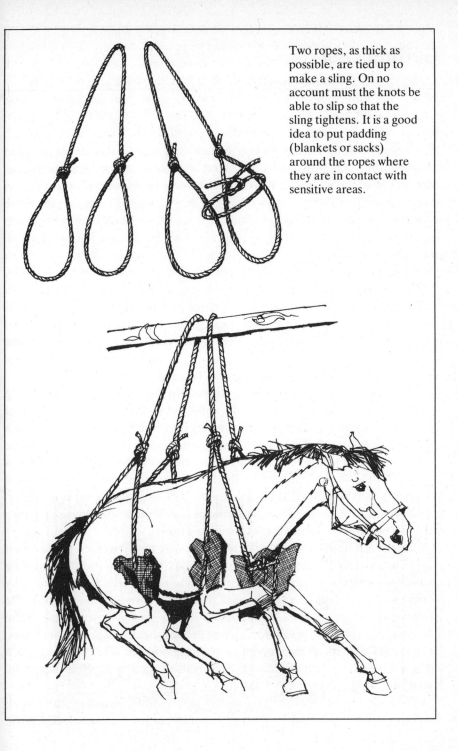

Two ropes, as thick as possible, are tied up to make a sling. On no account must the knots be able to slip so that the sling tightens. It is a good idea to put padding (blankets or sacks) around the ropes where they are in contact with sensitive areas.

to get a grip with the feet, so that they do not slip out from under the horse as it gets up. Asphalt or concrete floors should be grooved. Sloping walls are a good idea because they allow the feet to slide upwards, and not downwards as with vertical walls. Horizontal laths on the wall will provide a grip for the horse's feet. Three laths, with the top one 1–1.3 m from the ground, are sufficient. The straw should be banked up against the walls. This prevents the horse lying right up against the wall, as well as providing a purchase for the feet when it stands up. Problems experienced when trying to stand up can make horses reluctant to lie down. If a horse is making a concerted effort to get up, without panicking, give it time to gather its strength: sometimes that is all that is needed.

Bedding banked up against the walls to help prevent the horse getting cast. Ridges on the walls give the horse something to push against with its feet.

The horse which does not lie down

Horses can, up to a point, relax, rest and sleep standing up (this is made possible by the construction of the skeleton and the way the tendons work). However, it has been proven that lying down is essential to the horse's well-being. Complete decontraction cannot be achieved through long periods of standing, although there are stories told of horses which have never lain down in their lives.

There are several reasons why horses will not lie down. In many cases the cause is physical. Old horses may simply have become too stiff. Or a horse may, for example, be afraid of pain and difficulty experienced in getting up, due to degenerative changes in the hock. Horses which have, while lying down experienced breathing difficulties as a result of a pulmonary infection, also refuse to lie down.

The reasons are often psychological when, for example, a horse is new to a place, or feels insecure for any other reason. Nervous horses may be afraid to lie down if there are mice running round in the straw. Bad, dirty, damp bedding may be sufficient reason for a sensitive horse to remain on its feet.

Horses which pull back on their ropes, will not leave their stable or yard, and refuse to allow themselves to be led

Rubbing the headcollar off is not so much of a problem nowadays, because very few horses are kept in stalls. However, not only does this rather inhumane form of management still exist in some places, but horses also need to be tied up for other reasons. The first step in getting the headcollar off is stepping back in the stall. The horse steps back as far as its headcollar rope will allow, a habit which can have unpleasant consequences in stables with a narrow gangway behind the stalls, or another line of stalls on the other side of the gangway. Apart from the fact that they foul the gangway, these horses upset the others, get in the way, and cause kicking. The reason for this habit may be boredom, inquisitiveness or disgust at being perpetually tied up; or it may be impatience to be rid of the restriction of the tie rope. Use of the whip in this situation would be most inappropriate, and besides, a whip has no place in the stable. Hitting the horse with a muck fork or broom is also wrong (quite apart from the fact that a good horsemaster would never resort to such rough and ready methods). It is also incorrect to tie the horse up short. This will only lead to the horse doing its best to get rid of the headcollar completely. A rope or chain can be put across the back of the stalls, but this has the disadvantage that horses get into the habit of rubbing their hindquarters and tails on it. A bar can be used for the same purpose, but this incorporates the added risk that the horse will actually sit on it! It is a good idea to turn the horse so that it is facing the gangway – for short periods, of course.

One way of dealing with the problem is to use a self-tightening headcollar, which causes the horse to punish itself by putting pressure on the lower jaw when the horse steps back. It is also possible to obtain from the saddler a special kind of headcollar with an additional separate headpiece-cum-throatlatch, which fits the head better. The self-tightening headcollars are also useful for horses which break their headcollars on purpose, since this habit starts with the horse stepping backwards. It is more advisable, and better for the horse's training, to let the horse punish itself than to resort to a great, heavy headcollar which can lead to an accident.

From the horse's point of view, getting rid of the headcollar is an understand-

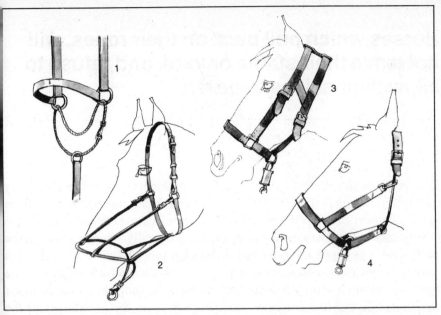

Headcollars nos. 1 and 2 serve to prevent the horse pulling back when tied up in a stall: the horse punishes itself when it does so. Types 3 and 4 make it impossible for the horse to get the headcollar off.

able reaction to being constantly tied up, but the consequences can be disastrous. Horses which wander up and down the gangway or into other horses' stalls at night upset the other horses, cause kicking, demolish stable fittings and knock everything off the windowsills. They may even start on the tack (which should have been put away in the tack-room) and take the saddle and bridle to bits, or gain access to the corn bin and gorge themselves, then go down with a severe case of colic.

With horses which slip their headcollars, simply doing up the throatlatch so tight that the horse can hardly breathe is definitely not the answer. It is better to get the saddler to make up a special headcollar along the lines of those illustrated, or of a similar type.

The same applies to horses which break loose when they are tied up in the gangway or in front of the stable for some purpose. It should be noted, however, that horses should be accustomed gradually to being tied up. Although young horses should learn to stand tied on both sides in the gangway, if there is any resistance it is not advisable to tie the horse on both sides straight away. Even though the horse may not stand so still, it has to start off by learning to stand tied on one side. It will come to accept the other side too with patience and calming words.

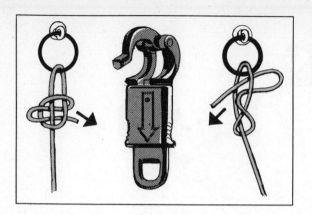

Two kinds of quick-release knot for use with a horse which is tied up. In the centre is a 'panic-clip', which can be undone by pulling.

If the horse pits all of its strength against being tied up, and panics to the point of risking injury to itself, then mistakes have certainly been made in its education. Paalman writes that with horses which refuse to stand tied, a piece of string which the horse can break easily should be inserted between the headcollar and the chain or rope. The horse will gradually give up the practice when it realises that it can break its rope easily. This is perhaps one possibility. The fact is that gentle, tactful handling, and powerful resistance can be equally effective in obtaining the horse's obedience. A really strong headcollar and, if necessary, a smack on the quarters can also have the desired effect. As is often the case when dealing with horses, deciding on the right method is a matter of equestrian tact.

Horses which will not leave their stables, or refuse to be led, are tiresome, and can make people look very silly. The handler tries to lead the horse out of the box, but it refuses to budge an inch, and stands obstinately like a wooden horse, with its legs straddled. Or else they have led the horse somewhere, and for no apparent reason, when there is nothing to frighten it, it clamps its feet down and refuses to move. Often, two fatal mistakes are made; *never*

1) turn and look the horse in the face unless you just want to calm it or coax it;

2) pull the horse, since the more you pull the more resistance the horse will offer, and you cannot hope to move half a ton or more of resisting horse. The bridle or headcollar will break, but the horse will not move a millimetre forwards.

The best course of action is to enlist an assistant to provide the necessary back-up. A short sharp tap, or whack if necessary, with the whip will show the horse that it must leave the box or that it must continue on its way. Talking quietly to the horse and praising it, and offering it some tasty morsel, will help get rid of any further resistance.

It is no good trying to pull a horse out of a stable if it does not want to come!

What should you do if you are alone? Making the horse go backwards a few steps can help, as can pushing it sideways with the shoulder, since getting it to move one step can provide the impetus to get it going again. Always turn the horse to the *right*, i.e. around its hindquarters. Never turn it left when leading it. Another method which will probably get the horse going is to drive it round on its forehand with a stick, as when doing preparatory schooling work in hand. Do not beat the horse or wrench it violently backwards: this will ruin its joints and spoil its good nature.

If your horse goes forward too impetuously and does not respond to a gentle or energetic tug on the headcollar rope (we will assume you lead your horse

The correct way to turn a horse is always to the right; if this method is used it cannot escape control. If the horse is turned to the left, the handler is liable to be taken off his guard and knocked over.

In order to lead a horse in a problem situation, it is a good idea to put the lead rope over the nose or through the mouth. Afterwards all you have to do is slacken the rope off

with a rope attached to its headcollar, as you should) then the lead rope can either be looped round the horse's nose or passed through its mouth. The latter method is more effective, but should only be used when absolutely necessary. Horses which have been trained to lead as foals and have normal temperaments will not usually present any problems later.

I wrote earlier that I assumed you never led your horse with just your hand on its headcollar. Never trust even the quietest horse: there is always something which can happen to upset it, and if you have ever been left swinging from a headcollar because you could not get your fingers out from underneath it, then you will know what can happen. This advice should be taken even more seriously when leading two horses.

Rearing while being led is also a bad form of disobedience. If a horse will not lead obediently, this deficiency in its education should be remedied immediately. For example you can get lead ropes which have a length of chain set into them just behind the panic clip (a quick-release clip). The purpose of the chain is to go through the horse's mouth. A normal headcollar rope can be used instead, but the horse cannot chew through a chain. A chain is also more effective. Carry a riding whip or stick in the left hand when leading, but hold it so that you can tap the horse on the nose with the handle – which is usually rigid – every time it is disobedient. And you must do just that; do it as if you mean it, the more it hurts the better! Hitting the horse like this, on the bony part of the nose above the nostrils is better than jabbing it in the mouth. You can also use your right hand to 'hook the horse back', but do not forget to 'give' with the hand again after you have done so. The horse must learn to walk along next to you on a very light contact, not rushing and not holding back. Talk to the horse, and use the commands 'Walk on' and 'Whoa' smartly and clearly. If the rearing continues in spite of your efforts to cure it, an anti-rear bit is a tried and tested aid. It is obvious from looking at this bit that it can be brutal in its action. It can cause dreadful injuries to the roof of the mouth. Take your time and try the gentle way first: as you know, the bad habits resulting from mistakes in the training take longer to cure than they do to pick up.

For horses which are difficult to catch, a practical method is to attach a short rope, about 20 to 30 cm long, to the headcollar. It does not hamper the horse while grazing, and you are in a better position to catch hold of the horse than with no rope at all. Many horses do not like being 'grabbed' by the head, so sudden movements of this kind should be avoided. You can catch hold of a rope faster than you can a headcollar. A knot in the end of the rope will give you more grip.

Problems in saddling and bridling

It is incredible how absurdly people also go about saddling and bridling their horses. When just about every mistake in the book has been made, and the horse has developed the corresponding bad habits, the problem is then a tiresome one. Everyone is familiar with the sight of a tiny person trying to put a bridle on an enormous horse. If a tall person can experience difficulties, someone small will be in a real predicament. The horse's head gets higher and higher, the person stands on tip-toe, yet he still cannot reach. The battle may end in anger and rough treatment. Take your time and work your way slowly and thoroughly along the horse's crest scratching it from withers to poll, like foals do to each other in the field. Try to find the spots where scratching makes the horse lower its head of its own accord to allow itself to be scratched, stroked and 'kneaded'.

Head-shyness is usually an acquired characteristic. It is caused by bad handling or a bad experience (or experiences), such as the use of force to put the bridle on, blows on the head, a badly put on or too tight twitch, bad experiences with the veterinary surgeon etc. It will take a long time to get rid of this habit – if indeed it can be cured. Traces of it will remain, and you must be careful not to react wrongly. The golden rule is no rapid movements, and a lot of tact and pursuasion. A horse which has become nervous in this way must have, or acquire, confidence in you. Whether the horse is afraid or not depends on the person who handles it, and how that person behaves.

As a general rule, the horse must be kept happy not only when it is being worked, but when the bridle is being put on. It is a good idea to talk to it constantly and to be generous with the titbits so that eventually it takes the bit willingly and allows the bridle to be pulled over its head and ears without pulling away. The important thing is to make the procedure as agreeable as possible for the horse, since it clearly finds it unpleasant.

Let us go through the normal procedure step-by-step. We begin with the horse wearing a headcollar, even in the stable, because, firstly it is easier to get hold of it, and secondly it is safer, especially if the horse panics. Care must be taken that there is nothing for the headcollar to get caught on. It must also fit properly, to ensure that the horse cannot get its foot caught in it.

The first step in putting the bridle on is to slide the reins over the neck, with the headcollar still on. The handler then positions himself on the left of the

56

horse, level with its neck, undoes the headcollar, and takes it off. He holds the
bit on the open palm of his left hand and pushes it gently but firmly into the
horse's mouth, pressing lightly with his forefinger and thumb if necessary. At
the same time, with his right hand, he pushes the headpiece of the bridle over
the right ear, holding the noseband up with it, by the nosepiece. The left ear is
then pulled through, and the noseband and throatlatch done up.

What should be done if the horse refuses to be bridled, and puts its head up
higher and higher? Always have a titbit with you, and give it to the horse before
you start to put the bridle on. The horse will want another. Few horses are so
contrary that they throw their head up straight away, but if it does so, give it
another titbit. Hold the horse with your right hand on its forehead, stroking it.
This hand is then ready to pull the bridle over the right ear, then the left. There
is no sense in trying to pull a horse's head down against its will. Once it has been
grabbed a few times, had the bit shoved roughly into its mouth, the noseband
wrenched tight, and both ears forced painfully through the bridle, any horse
will turn sour!

Usually the main problem is trying to push the bit into the mouth when the
horse is evading upwards with its head. If this is the case, instead of holding the
bridle by the headpiece, hold it in your right hand by the two cheek-pieces
about 10 cm above the bit. Stroke the right hand up and down the nose to try to
get the horse to comply. The left hand remains open, with the bit on it, ready to
push into the horse's mouth in the usual way. If the horse resists the right hand,
firm counter-pressure, given if necessary, is usually sufficient. Do not forget to
make much of the horse when you finally succeed in your aim. Incidentally,
some horses have extremely sensitive whiskers on their muzzles, but even if this
is the case, they should not be cut, because this would mean depriving the horse
of important organs of touch.

Horse playing up while being bridled.

Leave yourself plenty of time to put the bridle on. In winter, when the bit may be icy cold, no horse will particularly enjoy having such an instrument of torture put in its mouth. When doing up the noseband take care not to get any of the feeler hairs caught in the buckle. Horses can be very sensitive about this. We should also check the position of the bit in the horse's mouth. The corners of the lips should not be pulled upwards, but neither should the bit hang down so that it touches the tushes. A measuring stick carefully pushed through the mouth from side to side will give the width of the mouth, to which 1 cm should be added on either side. Particular care should be taken when fitting curb bits. The port should not be too high and the cheeks should not be too close to the sides of the face. The curb-chain should be turned (clockwise) until it is flat and should lie in the chin groove. A rubber curb guard may help if the horse is particularly sensitive in that area. There should be the same number of spare links on the right as on the left. Horses which have had bad experiences with pinching bits (e.g. worn eggbutt joints, or even narrow loose ring snaffles) may play up when it comes to putting the bit in. Remember also that with a drop noseband there should be room for three fingers between the noseband and the bridge of the nose, that the front part (nosepiece) should not be too long, that the buckle of the chin strap should not lie against the lips, and that the browband should not be too short or be fitted too high so that it pinches the base of the horse's ears. There should be room for the width of a hand underneath the throatlatch.

And now on to the subject of putting on the saddle. If the horse will not stand quietly to be saddled-up, it can be tied up with the headcollar fitted over the bridle. It goes without saying that when putting the headcollar over the bridle

(*Left*): The correct way to hold the bridle and bit to put them on. (*Right*): Correct fitting of a snaffle bridle with a drop noseband.

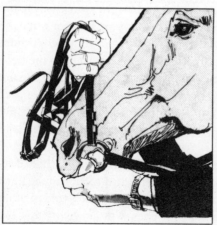 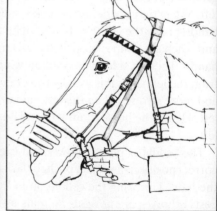

care should be taken that it does not press. Never tie a horse up by its bridle. It may be convenient, but apart from the fact that the horse can wreck the bridle without so much as a second thought, it can sustain nasty injuries to its mouth. If in the middle of a ride you have to tie the horse up for a while, put the headcollar on. At least, then, you can still ride home even if the headcollar gets broken.

A few words about the order in which the horse should be tacked up. If possible, tack up in the gangway next to the stables. In this case the saddle should be put on before the bridle. In the stable, things are done in the reverse order, supposing that the horse cannot or will not be tied up. If you start with the saddle, you may find the horse will keep running away from you round the box. This will develop into a bad habit which the horse will not forget. Putting the bridle on first is preferable, because then you can put your arm through the reins and keep control of the horse.

The question of whether to put the saddle on from the near-side or the off-side has long been a matter for discussion. In days gone by, when army horses were saddled up, with thick blankets underneath the saddle, putting the saddle on from the left presented no problem, because the blanket was carefully put on beforehand and checked for wrinkles. Moreover, army saddles were so stiff that the saddle flap could not get folded underneath. Not even the girth could get twisted. Nowadays the numnah, the saddle cloth or whatever (there is always something attached to the saddle) can get rucked up, the sweat flaps on the saddle can get folded under, and the lightweight girths now in use can become twisted. So why not put the saddle on from the off-side in the first place, since you will, in any case, have to go and check that side to make sure everything is lying flat and correctly?

However, horses do prefer being handled from the left and are more ready to accept someone approaching them from the left than from the right. As a general rule they tend to shy more often to the left and to turn more easily to the left. When they are being groomed, saddled or shod, they are happier when the handler is on the left than on the right of them. They are led from the left side, and when the whip is used while leading, it is used on the left (held in the right hand). The left side is the side on which they feel safe. In stalls, they are fed from the left side. It is usually the rider's right leg which applies the spur faster and more strongly than the left, and praise and titbits are usually given on the left. Hence the horse is, understandably, less tolerant on the right side than the left.

The saddle is placed slowly and carefully a few centimetres in front of its correct position, and then pushed back into position in the direction of the lie of the hair. Throwing the saddle on in haste and roughly is to be avoided at all costs – horses are nervous animals by nature. It goes without saying that the saddle area and the numnah should be clean. Praise your horse for standing quietly, or if it will not stand, praise it all the more to try to get it to do so. If the horse is tied on both sides it cannot move away so easily when the saddle is being put on. If it is tied to the wall, let it move sideways until it is standing next to the wall. It is also advisable to have somewhere to tie the horse in the stable, because horses often have to be tied up for one reason or another.

In stalls, the saddle is put on before the bridle. A common mistake is girthing up tight straight away. First let the horse come to terms with the fact that it has a saddle on, and only tighten the girths enough to keep the saddle in position. Put your spurs on and tidy up the mane and tail, and only when you have done this, gradually tighten the girths up. If you have a horse which blows itself up like a balloon, let out the girths a little on the off-side to make sure that they reach on the near-side when you come to do them up. With 'cold-backed' horses it is very dangerous to tighten the girths immediately. This habit is often caused by putting the saddle on incorrectly, especially if the horse has a sensitive back. A 'cold-backed' horse either bucks or refuses to go forwards and stands stubbornly rooted to the spot with its back humped. In extreme cases the horse may even go down. Lead the horse round a few times outside the stable, and do not tighten the girths until you can see that the horse has relaxed. If need be, get someone to give you a leg-up, and always sit down lightly in the saddle, never crash down. First walk round for a while with the girths fairly loose. Horses which blow themselves out should also be walked around for a few minutes. It is quite wrong to try to obtain things by force.

Difficulty with loading

Some horses will walk straight into the horsebox of their own accord, but they are in the minority. There are some ugly scenes to be witnessed at competitions when it comes to loading up. At the opposite end of the scale is the cowboy horse which, ready saddled and bridled, jumps of its own accord at least 80 cm on to the back of an open-topped lorry. Some horseboxes are constructed in such a way that they invite the horse to load, and recently, boxes have come on to the market which are equipped with a hydraulically operated system which can lower the whole body down to ground level. Some boxes are not so inviting, and this should be taken into consideration both when buying and when loading. You should try to make boxing a pleasant experience for the horse. Bad experiences while travelling will also influence it. All sorts of ghastly accidents have occurred, such as the floor collapsing and the horse's feet being dragged along the road, the horse going down in the box, being trampled on by other horses, getting caught up, breaking loose, jumping out, etc. etc.

It goes without saying that the ramp must be solid and not shake when the horse steps on it. It must not be too steep, and it should be covered with straw. It should not be dark inside the box, which should be as roomy as possible to encourage the horse to enter. It should also smell clean, and the roof should not be too low, since this makes the horse feel restricted.

Sufficient time must be allowed for loading the horse, and there should be no chasing and shouting. Practise loading at home before the day of the journey. Make the horse familiar with the box, feed it frequently inside the box if necessary. Wait till the horse is hungry, so that it is pleased to go into the horsebox for a feed. If you have a box which takes more than one horse, you can perhaps find another horse which can be taken into the box first to encourage your own horse to enter.

If none of these methods work, what then? Only one thing is certain: you can no more pull a horse into a horsebox by its headcollar than you can drag it out of the stable against its will, as has already been explained. Neither can you push it into the horsebox. In order to avoid potential problems from the outset, and also to leave the horse in no doubt as to the fact that it must go in the box, it is advisable to use the best method from the start. Of course you can first try blindfolding the horse, or leading it round and round in circles until it loses its bearings. Of course you can try thrashing it to make it go in, or backing it up the

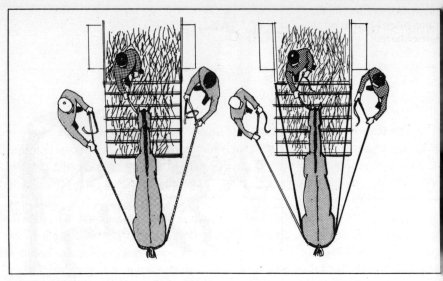

Loading with a rope or two lunge lines.

ramp, or riding it in if the box is open at the top, but all these ways can go
wrong, and you will finish up with a horse which is even more resistant. It has
learnt that it can get away with it – and it will make good use of such knowledge!
So why not do it properly from the start?

Take two lunge lines (two strong ropes will do), and attach them one to each
side of the horsebox. The other ends of the ropes are each held by an assistant.
The two assistants each run the lunge they are holding around the horse's
quarters, and in so doing cross over to the opposite side of the box. The horse is
'enclosed' by the two lunge lines around its quarters. Another assistant, prefer-
ably the one whom the horse knows best, holds the headcollar rope, and a
handful of hay, a carrot or a similar delicacy. A fourth assistant stands behind
with a whip at the ready. The horse is then pulled into the box by the two
assistants with the lunge lines, while the one with the whip drives and pushes
from behind. It is important that the horse cannot jump off the side of the
ramp. If possible the trailer should be driven up to the door of the stable so that
one side, at least, can be blocked off.

Often the horse gets as far as the bottom of the ramp but refuses to step onto
it. Lift up first one fore foot and then the other, with the assistants pulling hard
on the lunge lines at the same time. Once you have overcome this hurdle, the
horse will keep going. There should be no shouting, but rather encouragement
and plenty of praise! It is very important to shut the tail gate as soon as the horse
is in. Not until this has been done should the horse be tied up. During the
journey you should check that everything is alright. Once the horse has learned

Getting an assistant to place the front feet on the ramp often helps to get the horse started.

that entering the box presents no problem, two men with their hands joined behind its quarters will suffice to push it in (with a third holding the headcollar rope, of course). Once the horse is used to being loaded with two lunge lines, the same system but with only one rope or lunge line can be tried.

When loading up after dark, remember that those horses which have a particular tendency to shy at things on the ground ('ground-shy') react very violently if they see the beam of a torch on the ground in front of them. You should check your horse's reaction before shining the torch on the ramp or inside the box to show it what is there. Lamps which illuminate a large area are better, but even so you should avoid shining any light on the horse from the front, since it may be dazzled and unable to see where it is treading. Furthermore there should be no reflective metal objects shining or glinting in the vicinity. All in all it is better to park the horsebox somewhere lighter and not light up the inside at all, because horses find this disturbing. Diffused lighting is quite sufficient, and is more pleasant for the horse than a bright light which can trigger off violent reflex actions. With bright lights there are often moving shadows on the wall and ground, and these too can be a source of irritation.

Problems during unloading can also be avoided by being careful. Unload nervous horses first. Obviously, if it is possible to turn the horse round in the box, this should be done and it can then be unloaded forwards. Ramps should be solid and not too steep. When backing down, the horse should be supported on either side by an assistant to prevent it stepping over the side of the ramp.

It is often sufficient for two helpers to join hands behind the horse's hindquarters. Lifting up one of the fore feet also makes it easier for the horse to step on the ramp. (*Right*) Off-loading.

Speak soothingly to the horse and back it down slowly. Do not turn it round on the ramp, because the next time it will anticipate this and turn of its own accord – rather too fast for comfort! In so doing it can easily step over the edge of the ramp and injure itself.

Problems on the lunge

Before dealing with the subject of bad habits in the ridden horse, a few words about lungeing. It is beyond the scope of this study to deal with this matter in detail, however, there are certain situations of which horses take advantage in order to misbehave, and it is these we shall consider.

Whether you lunge in a cavesson with side-reins, a chambon or over-head check reins, with a saddle, lungeing roller, long reins, or simply a lunge rein attached to a headcollar (though the latter does not count as lungeing in the true sense of the term) is not a matter for discussion here, though it is significant, since lungeing, like riding, can be done either professionally or amateurishly. A horse can be put on its forehand instead of on its haunches, and it can have its mouth ruined and its neck and poll made stiff instead of supple.

It goes without saying that a young horse, which is always liable to present problems, should never be lunged without at least one assistant. For the first few days the assistant leads the horse by the cheekpiece, of the cavesson or short hand rein on the inside. The horse should learn during this period to keep to the line of the circle and to obey the commands. How to give these commands should already be known. The important thing is that the horse learns that it cannot simply do as it pleases. It is difficult to sort out an unruly horse on the lunge without an assistant: rough treatment is to be avoided at all costs. A properly marked out circle has been found to be useful, and if a 'lungeing ring' is not available a boundary can be improvised with straw bales. Whatever is used, the horse should not be able to injure its legs on it. Things are much easier if there are two of you, and you can prevent the practice of turning in at the halt and walking towards the lunger. This practice is widespread, and is incorrect. The horse must remain halted on the track until the lunger walks up to it. It is therefore necessary to ensure from the outset that calmness and obedience prevail and that no insubordination is tolerated. The early education will be reflected later in the work under saddle. It also makes reschooling easier if there is a sound foundation to refer back to.

Vices Under Saddle

Bad habits in the ridden horse

The number of books and studies on the subject of equine psychology is not very great. Only occasionally does one find in the many books about riding and dealing with horses a few random and generalised notes of a psychological nature. When the horse lost its importance as a means of transport and a working animal, the value of a thorough study of the subject of equine psychology also disappeared. It became a purely scientific study with no practical application since the horse has now become an instrument of sport rather than a necessity. Hence this section of the book, about misbehaviour under saddle, is mainly based on experience.

We have already discussed the dictionary definition of 'vice', the deviation from the normal behaviour pattern which affects man's utilisation of the horse. Here again many of these behaviour problems are the result of wrong handling by man, either in the form of mistakes made in training, or unintentional bad treatment resulting from ignorance of the inevitable consequences and possibly also of the quirks of that particular animal. It is often difficult to draw the line between the horse's predisposition to play up, and man's incorrect handling of the horse: the two tend to overlap. It is almost impossible to prescribe a universal 'remedy' for hard-boiled offenders in particular, and it has been shown all too frequently that an unorthodox method can effect a quicker and more fundamental cure than the general advice given in a book.

It must be accepted that there are ways of curing or eliminating bad habits which seem very much at variation with the principles of riding and psychological knowledge. For example, I remember that I once had to ride a restless, hysterical mare on a trek of hundreds of kilometres through Russia, because my own horse had broken loose during some shooting and run away. The mare, of whom I had a very poor opinion, belonged to an officer, who had never got on with her. She jogged permanently, never walked, and was consequently very lean. She danced up and down, without advancing, in a 'sewing machine trot' and an equally unpleasant, scrabbling canter. The prospect of riding this 'goat' on a ride lasting several days and covering a long distance through enemy country seemed unbearable, the more so since in this case one also had one's own salvation to think about. Most riders will be able to give me a list of the ways to deal with such a horse, but these were no more help than the idea that sooner or later she would have to tire, the more so since she already had several days march behind her when I was obliged to take her over. What was to be done? I did what would make any rider blush to tell: in my despair I screamed at the poor animal and gave her the most horrific jabs in the mouth and, with the spurs, in the flanks. After a while the shouting was sufficient by itself, and, eventually, just drawing breath to shout did the trick. To sum up, I reached my destination with a mare who had put on weight and was externally unrecognisable. She would walk, had a nice, easy trot and canter, and was content. All this story goes to show is that there are other ways of doing things than those prescribed by the instruction manuals or handed down from experience.

Another problem is 'restiveness'. Congenital viciousness, which is included in this term, has now mostly been bred out. Restiveness (i.e. exceptional continued resistance) resulting from inexpert handling, makes systematic use of the horse impossible, and can only be successfully eliminated if there are no serious physical shortcomings and the horse is not asked to do something it is not capable of. Pain resulting from excessive demands being made can lead to resistance, either because the horse has, for example, a pain in the back, or because it is constantly having its head forced into an almost physically impossible position.

Spohr says on the subject of handling problem horses: 'A person who tries to correct problem horses without speaking to them will not get on so well.' This is true: You should talk soothingly to your horse not only when you are trying to get it to do something, but also when it has done something well. Horses like to be praised, they like to receive acknowledgement of something done right, and likewise they can be deeply upset by a reproof, since they can distinguish between different tones of voice.

Restiveness is easier to cure if the horse's lack of enthusiasm for its work can be overcome and its forward urge re-established. Hack out with a friend in the country, potter about without making any big demands, and take your horse out in hand to graze; give your horse a holiday, as it were. This does not mean, however, that you should let it get up to mischief when you are out riding – even giving your horse a free rein has its limits. However, the limits should be imposed with a kind, soft hand, without fuss, and with gentle firmness and enormous patience.

Refusing to stand while being mounted

This is a clear case of faulty education: the horse will not stand still while being mounted, but creeps backwards, spins round, tries to go forwards, perhaps tries to bite, tenses up, and/or rears. What should be done?

Do not attempt to tackle the problem on your own. It takes a lot of patience and calmness to make a horse with this problem obedient again. An assistant should stand at the horse's head, in front of it. When backing a young horse, the best thing is for the assistant to be armed with a scoop of oats, but when reschooling a spoiled horse all he needs to do is make sure the horse stands still, and give it the odd titbit. In extreme cases, the assistant stands on the right of the horse, holds the horse's right cheekpiece (not the reins) with his right hand and with his left hand hangs on to the right stirrup leather (at the top, by the buckle) to prevent the saddle slipping, or being pulled, sideways. It is also his job to place the stirrup (turned the right way round) on the rider's foot. He may

Assistance with mounting. It is not essential to have quite so many helpers, but you do need two or three.

also turn the horse's head slightly to the right, which is what the rider should do anyway when he mounts. It is important that the rider sits down softly, and does not suddenly weigh down hard on the horse's back, and that the horse is spoken to constantly and rewarded with bread, sugar or pieces of apple. Do not be content with mounting once, practise doing so repeatedly, because there is hardly anything worse than, for example, being stuck in the country with a horse which will not let you get on it.

Once you have mounted, with assistance, ride forwards immediately. Make sure you are sitting correctly, sort out your gloves, clothes and reins, talk to your horse, and, as has already been said, keep mounting and dismounting until your horse stands. The legendary riding master, Stensbeck, used to light a cigar and read a newspaper, and his horse had to be able to stand still while he did so. Young horses, however, should not be made to stand still for long periods, firstly because they have less patience, and secondly because of the unaccustomed weight on their backs. Nevertheless, they still have to learn to stand.

If you do have to tackle this problem without assistance, try to position the horse up against a wall. Although this is feasible in the school, it is rarely possible to do so when you are out in the country. So what should you do then? You may be able to get another rider to position his horse alongside yours, on the right. If so, shorten your right rein, bend the horse's head gently to the right, and make sure you get on without digging the horse in the tummy with your toe: some horses object to this! Stand very close to the horse when you mount so that your centre of gravity coincides approximately with that of the horse from the outset, and slide into the saddle – do not crash down into it! Do not forget to praise the horse. And then practise mounting and dismounting: walk the horse forward a few steps and then start again from the beginning. There is a maxim in show horse judging: a horse goes as it stands. As well as referring to how a horse moves, this can also be applied to the horse's behaviour under saddle. An obedient horse will have learnt to stand, so its behaviour while being mounted is representative of its behaviour in general.

In days gone by people used to mount their horses with a 'leg-up'. This was not only for reasons of convenience, but simply because horses stand more calmly without someone pulling them down and twisting them round on one side, swinging one leg through the air, digging a toe into their tummy, and finally crashing over 70 or 80 kg down on their loins.

That well-known feature, the mounting block, also evolved for reasons other than pure convenience. A great horseman of recent times, Otto Lörke, used to mount from a mounting block in the gangway between the stables (and, incidentally, he used to 'loosen up' his horse with a few steps of piaffe as soon as he reached the school). So accepting a leg-up on to a horse which has learnt to stand should not make you feel you are being lazy, or cheating, particularly if it actually helps to make the horse stand. If your horse is too tall, you can also let out the left stirrup leather a few holes to make it easier to mount. Stirrup leathers are also available which incorporate a 'low position' for easy mounting. With mares which dislike being girthed up tight, it is essential to have an assistant on the right of the saddle to ensure that it does not slide to the left and then under the horse's belly. Obviously it is a good idea for the assistant to place the stirrup in the correct position under the sole of the boot, because fishing around with the foot for the stirrup can sometimes irritate the horse and encourage it to fidget.

In the days when the big herds of horses in East Prussia used to be accompanied by herdsmen, it was inevitable that these young lads, who had been chosen for their horse sense, would succumb to the temptation to ride some of the young horses. When these horses later came to be broken in, valuable preliminary work had already been done, since they had already had a person on their backs, nothing dreadful had happened to them, they had no need to be afraid, and so there were no problems. Breeders who appreciate the task the trainer faces also take the trouble (though not only for this reason) to prepare the horse from an early age for the day it will have to tolerate a person on its back. A child is legged up casually on to the horse in the stable or corridor, and, because the child does not weigh much and the scene is so informal, the event makes less of an impression on the horse, and it learns quite incidentally to carry a man on its back.

What should we do if we have a horse which has never had anyone on its back – no herdsman and no child – and in addition it is sensitive, nervous and not at all keen on letting anything of the sort take place? We should 'play around' with the horse, for example, when we have just given it its feed we should lean against its left side with one arm over its back, patting it in different places, talking to it and putting weight on its back. We should put a saddle cloth or numnah on its back and pat it with our hand. Later we can put a saddle on top of it. The horse must be allowed to sniff everything. At first the saddle is only laid on the horse's back, and the horse is praised, patted and given food. The saddle is then taken off and put back on again, and at some point the girth is passed round the horse's belly, and then done up. The horse is taken for a walk – with the saddle on – and the saddle is patted and the stirrups pulled down, and then run up again. When the horse accepts all this calmly, we can start lungeing. Here again the horse may panic, because the stirrups bang against the saddle even though they are, of course, run up out of the way and secured.

I am not very keen on the idea of putting a sandbag on the horse's back. It is not so much the weight which alarms the horse, but rather the fact that there is something on its back. The primitive fear inherited from its ancestors comes to the fore: the horse thinks it could be a beast of prey about to bite it at that vulnerable point, the withers, with fatal results. A better course of action is to allay the horse's fear so that it begins to understand that the whole thing is just a game, in which the person who gives the horse nice things to eat and chats to it, suddenly sits on it, without anything nasty happening. Get someone to lift you up against the horse, hang on the saddle, lie across the saddle, and then lift your leg over the saddle. Keep your upper body horizontal at first, then gradually sit up. A bowl of food held under the horse's nose can be very helpful at this point. If problems arise during backing, it is advisable to work in the stable, and not in the corridor. Never tie the horse up for this purpose. Be satisfied with small beginnings, and never ask for too much at once if you have had problems with the horse. Never forget the basic principle that the horse must be kept happy. You will never get on the horse's back against its will, unless you do so rodeo-style, and that is not exactly what we are aiming at! If, after you have mounted the horse for the first time, you do encounter resistances, your assistants should ensure that this does not happen again. Once a horse has discovered that it does not have to tolerate a man on its back it will soon learn how to stop people getting on it. The helpers must keep hold of the horse at all costs. It is best if the rider dismounts immediately, the horse is calmed down, and the whole procedure begun again from the beginning, rather than a fight developing between horse and rider. To start with you should always be more careful than may be necessary, so as to avoid incidents or to nip any problems in the bud. A lead rein, not attached to the bit ring, can be helpful. Once a horse has managed to escape, it will do so again.

Shying

Before we refer to shying as a bad habit we should understand some of the horse's behaviour patterns. Horses flee from things which could mean danger, and many of the ridden horse's reactions bear witness to this instinct. Some people say that horses orientate themselves by smell, and that they cannot see clearly. Others say horses see everything in an enlarged form, and that they take fright easily for this reason. The latter explanation is illogical, since if the horse sees things bigger, it must see everything bigger, so that things are still the same size in relation to each other, and there is no cause for alarm.

Horses which do not know each other, sniff each other's noses, necks and genital areas. A horse will do this – as Grzimek has shown – even if the other horse is a stuffed one. The stuffed horse will be sniffed, and even nibbled tenderly on its leg and neck; it will be greeted with a whinny, and, if need be, zealously defended against adversaries. It is interesting that a life-size painting of a horse provoked the same reactions, but that the interest disappeared if the image was greatly simplified, or abstract, and so no longer life-like. Hence we know that horses recognise each other and their environment not only by smell (that is, predominantly through information provided by the nose), but also by sight. The horse's eye sees in a different way from a man's eye, so we need to concern ourselves with this subject in depth. It will provide explanations for many reactions and the 'misbehaviour' which these can result in.

The horse can perceive the slightest movement. This is particularly evident in the case of circus liberty horses, for whom the slightest upward movement of the whip or a slight movement of the trainer's hand serves to transmit a command. The expression on the trainer's face, however, is not noticed by the horse. It makes no difference whatsoever if the trainer smiles when he says 'No!' and grimaces when he says 'Good boy'. Yet if he should decide suddenly to wear a large hat in addition to his usual clothes, this could create complications.

When man sees an object, it is with both eyes together, and the image is graphic and sharp. The axes of the eyes run parallel to one another. Everything which lies to the side of these axes is not sharp, and the further round to the side it is, the less sharp it is. The field of vision is restricted. The horse's eye, on the other hand, looks sideways, and not forwards. The axes of the eyes point in very different directions. This means that the horse's eye cannot see any given

75

object as clearly as man can, but it sees things fairly well and in a much wider field. Probably the horse has an even view of the horizon almost all the way around it. This is a very wide field of vision (like a 'wide angle' lens) compared with that of man ('normal lens'), and of a bird of prey ('telephoto lens').

The position of the horse's eyes has evolved through adaptation to the steppe environment. The oval shape of the pupil goes with the position of the eye, and facilitates the all-round vision. An oval pupil can also tolerate brighter light than a round pupil because the difference between the fully open position and the completely shut position is greater. The cornea of the horse's eye has a greater curvature from top to bottom than from side to side, which causes a certain distortion of objects: a dot looks like a stick. A fluorescent layer behind the retina increases the light sensitivity of the horse's eye in poor lighting conditions. This means that the horse's eye can see much better than the human eye in darkness. Blendinger summarises the horse's vision as follows ('Wilhelm Blendinger: *Psychologie und Verlalteusweise des Pferdes*, Erich Hoffmann Verlag. Heidenheim/Brenz, 1977', p. 214f. Reproduced by kind permission of the publisher.):

1. The horse does not see worse or better than man, but quite differently, so that we have only a limited conception of the actual way it sees.
2. The horse sees, relatively well, almost 360° around it, but it does not see any one point as clearly as man does.
3. Since the horse is unable to look with both eyes at any one point, perception of form and perspective, evaluation of distance, and so assessment, is probably harder for the horse than for man.
4. The horse is used to looking at lots of things all at once, and finds it difficult to concentrate on one object in front of it. Hence part of a jumper's training is learning to see correctly.

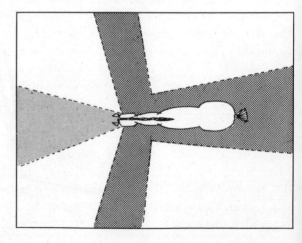

When the head is straight, the horse's field of vision comprises *either* the area bordered by lines in front *or* the sectors on either side *and* to the rear. It does *not* comprise the front area and the two side areas at the same time (according to SMYTHE).

5. The horse is capable of adapting to far greater extremes of light and darkness than man. However, it is thought to take longer to adapt to sudden changes in lighting.
6. The horse's ability to perceive movement is superior to that of man.
7. The horse can distinguish the colours red, yellow, green and blue, but it sees them in a different intensity to man: it sees yellow and green more clearly than blue and red.

A horse will not fully accept things it is afraid of until it has sniffed them and touched them with its nose repeatedly. It will turn away and then come back and examine the object again, just as carefully. Fear is accompanied by curiosity. Usually, in the inner struggle, it is curiosity which wins – though the battle may flare up again later! Certain smells cause intense fear in horses, as they do in many living creatures. They include blood, smoke, and smells which bring back memories of the veterinary surgeon. There is a saying that the horse thinks with its nose. Pronounced affections or aversions of horses to people are often caused by something the horse has smelt. A frightened person smells differently from one who goes up to the horse confidently and briskly, quite apart from the fact that he walks differently.

The horse makes observations with its ears, as well as its eyes and nose. It has extraordinarily fine hearing. Its ears are in constant movement, and are continually locating sounds which man often cannot hear. A horse will spot a rustling leaf or a deer in a cornfield, without the rider having heard a thing. With very nervous or sensitive horses, the rider must be constantly on his guard for the horse being startled by something. Riding along without paying attention can be disastrous. Be ready to shorten your reins if necessary, and get used to gripping with your knees. When you are riding on a loose rein, for example when out hacking, get into the habit of holding the reins in the left hand, so that

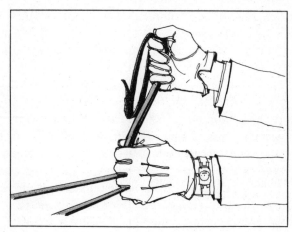

When the reins are held in one hand, they can be shortened quickly, as shown, in an emergency.

when they have to be shortened suddenly, the right hand can be used to pull them through the left to the correct length. With this method you first get your horse under control and then separate your reins. This is better than trying to take up the reins with both hands in a hurry, because they will get tangled up.

As we have seen, the horse becomes aware of things it thinks it ought to be frightened of before the rider. Often the rider can and must anticipate what could make the horse shy. If you cannot avoid riding past a frightening object, you must prepare the horse, and not transmit your own uncertainty, or even fear, to it. On the other hand you should not be any more energetic than necessary, because this too will be noticed by the horse.

Let us assume that you have seen a man sitting on a bench reading a newspaper, and your horse has not yet seen him. Your horse will not notice him until he moves, and then it will take fright and jump away. It will only go a few steps, however, until it has established the necessary 'flight distance', then it will stop and try to ascertain what the frightening thing is. There is no point in punishing the horse for jumping away, because you cannot beat a reflex action, such as this, out of a horse. The horse is simply obeying one of the laws of nature, since its ability to perceive movement is obviously superior to that of the human eye. It sees objects which move suddenly particularly clearly – and particularly fast. This rapidity of perception, which is far greater than that of man, can result in the horse jumping abruptly to one side before the rider has seen the object. Obviously the horse should not be praised for doing so either! The best course of action is to anticipate what might arise.

In contrast to the horse's reaction to fear-inspiring sudden movements, is its behaviour in respect of stationary objects such as farm machinery, barns, piles of wood or whatever. These it approaches snorting, tense, and ready to spin round or jump aside at any moment. In other words it will not leap sideways by reflex action as it would with something that suddenly moves 'out of the blue'. Instead it will react more like a mounted reconnaissance patrol on the edge of a forest suspected of harbouring the enemy. When it is far enough away for safety it will suddenly turn round, to entice the suspected enemy out of the ambush.

So what do horses shy at, and what should the rider do about it once he knows what the visual causes are? Young, inexperienced horses are generally more nervous, but also more curious. Unfamiliar objects are viewed with great suspicion from a long way off. It is advisable to get a less nervous or more experienced horse to take the lead. Once you have persuaded your horse to approach the object of its mistrust, you have scored a major victory. When riding a young or nervous horse out hacking, ride all the time with a very firm seat in anticipation of something upsetting it. Possible causes are an animal in the undergrowth, on the edge of the forest or in a cornfield, or a paper or plastic bag blown by the wind or showered with loose soil as the horse goes past. The only thing you can do about this is put the horse properly 'on the aids', with a controlled contact with the bit, put your knees against the saddle and ride in sitting trot with the upper body leaning backwards slightly (never use rising trot in these circumstances). So if you are trotting or cantering along the edge of a wood, if possible leave plenty of space between yourself and the wood, and always have your horse well and truly 'on the aids'. Moreover, if you go past a place where your horse has shied before, you can assume it will do so again – even years later!

Jumping sideways is the mildest form of shying, and can also result from overfreshness: some horses will take every opportunity to use their strength. There is little point in jabbing the horse in the mouth: the next time the horse will react even more violently because it will also be afraid of the pain. It is better to stop and walk past the object a few times, so as to show the horse there is nothing to get excited about, and to praise it when it gradually forgets its excitement. Over-freshness and shying can also be an opportunity to stretch the muscles, like a child who has been sitting for too long in one place and finally has to find an outlet for his energy. Horses such as these should be ridden forwards to get rid of the surplus energy. Some horses pretend to shy so that they can spin round – in the direction of home. On the way back they usually find fewer things to shy at!

Any number of things can cause a horse to get excited: a person sitting on a bench at the side of the road reading a newspaper, a pram parked in front of the bench, perhaps with a parasol, a person bending down behind a tree collecting mushrooms, a skier gliding across the snow, a pile of wood, etc. etc.

Prams, umbrellas, parasols, handbarrows or any other common, everyday object can cause a horse to shy.

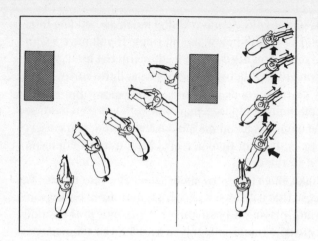

(*Left*): Incorrect position for passing an object which the horse has shied at.
(*Right*): The correct way is to turn the horse away and push it past forwards and sideways. In this way it does not step backwards and so evade even more.

What should you do if the shying has developed into an out and out resistance, and the horse keeps stopping and refusing to pass things, even if you can find another horse to give you a lead? A well-timed crack with the whip may help – but the horse must not be thrashed. Turn the horse away from the object of its fear, and try to push it past the object sideways in a leg-yield. Be definite with your aids: any uncertainty will be transmitted to your horse. Remember that the horse's eye sees objects in a less distorted fashion if they are not in front of it, so turn its head away.

If none of these methods helps, get off and lead the horse. Do take the reins over its head, however. This is important, because it gives you better control. Be logical and systematic: reins in the right hand when the object is on the left,

The correct way to lead a horse. Note the lack of stiffness in the arm, which is bent slightly; the reins are separated by the index- and middle-fingers, and the end of the reins is held under the thumb. If this method is used, a shying horse can be brought back under control promptly.

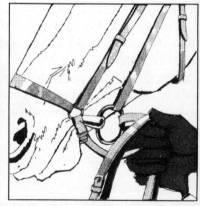

hold the ends of the reins under your thumb with the index and middle finger separating the reins a hand's breadth below the bit rings. If you have a whip, hold it in your left hand, and if you need to use it, do so on the hindquarters. You should always position yourself between the object and the horse, so that it cannot push you away or even knock you over. If the object the horse is frightened of is on the right, you should lead the horse with your left hand and hold the whip in your right hand. As has already been mentioned, you must not pull on the reins: the horse is stronger than you are! Moreover, you must not face the horse and look it in the eye.

If the horse does not make much fuss, stay in the saddle, be very patient and let it walk up to the object so that it can see that there is nothing to be afraid of. However, although you are playing a passive role, sit firmly in the saddle, because the horse may try to spin round suddenly. The rider's legs should serve to show the horse that no misbehaviour will be tolerated.

Training at home in the school can help prepare the horse for these situations. Put a piece of paper – an open newspaper or a sheet of wrapping paper – on the ground, near the track, so that pieces of sand etc. fall on it and make a noise as the horse goes past. Also place a table with objects on it in the school. Someone can rustle pieces of paper on the table, or a gust of wind can blow a sheet of paper away or turn a page in a book – and do not forget the umbrella! Get someone to stand in the school with an umbrella, flourishing it and moving it about. A baby's pram can also be used for training. In fact there are numerous possibilities. You should also get your horse used to noise.

It is quite possible, through systematic training, to get your horse used to the unusual. Riding is not just about doing certain specified dressage exercises, or jumping higher and higher courses in shorter and shorter times. We also have the chance to go for rides in the country. It is amazing but true that nowadays horses shy less at tractors and cars than they do at cows or sheep in a field, and a jet fighter has a far less frightening effect than a bird flying out of the undergrowth!

Horses which shy excessively at things on the ground are sure to be suffering from a visual defect. As an experiment, a white line was drawn in the grass of a field which some horses knew well. The horses jumped over the line. It can also happen that a horse jumps over the imprint left on the floor of the school by a pole or cavalletti. You cannot change the fact that a horse is ground-shy, but you can train it not to embarrass you all the time by refusing to go through puddles for example.

Refusing to go into water

Refusing to go into water does not mean that the horse is water shy. In general, horses are not water shy. However, an innocent puddle in the stable corridor is greeted with tension and frantic snorting, especially by young horses. Washing a young horse's feet for the first time can create problems if it has not had it done as a foal. Even the sight of the bucket arouses suspicion. The cold, the water running down its legs and the resulting puddle on the ground can trigger off resistance. Start with the hind legs, because horses are usually more willing to allow these to be washed than their fore legs. Use a sponge, not a hard brush, and if possible do not use very cold water. If you encounter difficulties, have someone hold up the fore foot on the same side, and be content with small beginnings. You should try not to let the puddle on the ground get too large.

The horse will get used to the water gradually. You can then do the same thing using a hose-pipe. First, with the water turned down low, accustom the horse to being hosed from the knee and hock downwards. You should only increase the flow very gradually. Take the opportunity to lead your horse through the puddle, be it in the corridor, in the stable, or in front of the stable. Also accustom your horse to going through puddles caused by storms. However, you should never confuse your horse when you are out hacking, by trying to get it to go through pools of water which are deep or have no proper bottom (like the pools to be found in boggy fields), and where it could get a nasty surprise and encounter difficulties. Once your horse has had a bad experience it will not trust you again and will refuse to go through the next harmless puddle it meets. It can sometimes be helpful to dismount and lead a horse through a puddle, or to follow another horse through. On no account must you get the horse worked up if it refuses to go through. Wait until you can get another horse to lead yours through.

You can then progress to streams and ponds. If in spite of all your efforts and patience you cannot get the horse to go through, you should go back to the same spot with lunge lines or rope and at least three helpers. As described in the chapter on loading, the lunge lines are put around the horse's quarters. Each assistant pulls his lunge line tight around the quarters, while you sit on top and keep the horse straight to prevent it dodging out to one side. If necessary you can get someone to help from behind. Be positive, but without shouting or thrashing the horse. However, one sharp blow with the whip can be given at the

Two assistants in front with a rope or lunge line, and possibly a third helper behind (perhaps equipped with a whip in certain cases), will succeed in making any horse go into the water.

point when it seems most necessary. Once you have managed to get the fore feet in the water, let the horse stand for a while to get used to the feeling (obviously it must not be allowed to step backwards). This will make the next stage easier. Repeat the exercise two or three times, and then be satisfied for the time being. If the stream is not very wide, the horse may take an enormous leap over it. You must be prepared: do not jab the horse in the mouth, yield the reins immediately.

If you have previously trained the horse to allow its feet to be washed, it often helps if an assistant pours water from the pond or stream down the horse's fore legs while it is standing on the bank. Try not to start your horse rearing. If it does so, instead of putting the lunge lines round the quarters, the assistants should attach them at the front and hang onto them tightly to stop the horse going up. The horse will probably refuse all over again as soon as it is taken to a different spot. Energetic use of legs and voice will ensure that it is in no doubt as to the fact that it must go into or through the water here, just as it did at the other spot. Get someone to give you a lead with another horse if necessary. Eventually this spot too will be accepted, and gradually the horse will learn that the rider will not give in.

Many horses start pawing the water with their fore legs. This is thought to be to test the depth. It is also suggested that this is the horse's way of expressing its fear of the unknown in the water, or of expelling an imaginary source of danger. Very often, however, I feel it is just a game, the horse's way of showing it likes the water. Horses without riders on their backs also go into water if they get the chance. The only thing which prevents a horse going into water voluntarily is fear.

Often, however, pawing the water is also a prelude to trying to lie down, which some horses can do in a very short space of time. There have been frequent cases of horses disappearing into the water complete with their riders At the first sign that your horse's knees are starting to buckle you must take instant action in the form of a powerful upward jerk combined simultaneously with a jab with both spurs and loud use of the voice. Not all horses have this habit. You will know if your own horse is that way inclined, but you should be wary of horses you do not know.

Obviously, when accustoming a horse to water you do not seek out the most difficult places to cross the stream or pond. Your horse must have confidence in you. Starting with small obstacles – in this case puddles and streams etc. – will teach it to take your decisions on trust. The horse is quite simply afraid of the unknown ground which is concealed by the layer of water. The horse transmits to the ground, through its foot, about ten times as much weight per square centimetre as man does, so that the risk of sinking into the ground is correspondingly greater. The rider must communicate to the horse the assurance that nothing will happen to it in the water. This obedience, based on trust, will later enable the horse to go over a jump (a small one to start with) in the water.

Ditches too must be introduced gradually. Under normal circumstances a horse has no difficulty in clearing a water-filled ditch two metres wide, which is no more than an extended canter stride. So what prevents it from doing so? It may be that the sparkling, reflective surface of the water confuses the horse. On the other hand, there have been cases of horses jumping ditches without a rider.

It is very easy nowadays to construct artificial ditches of any width. Plastic sheets can even be used instead of water. It is advisable to make the jump easier for the horse to start with, either by placing a small brush fence on the take-off side, or by putting a low pole across the middle.

Horses used to be loose-schooled in so-called 'jumping lanes'. These are not so common nowadays, but you can improvise a similar facility by using jump wings. This can also be used to accustom the horse to jumping artificial ditches made with foil. The width of the ditches has been shown to be of secondary importance. 'Ground-shy' horses will be more of a problem, and will probably never be reliable. In such cases the rider must appreciate that it does not do the horse any good to confront it suddenly with a ditch in a competition or out hunting. All too often this leads to a very unedifying spectacle.

For the rider who simply hacks about, it makes no difference whether or not the horse will go through puddles, over ditches and into ponds. If it will not, he will simply have to ride round the obstacle in question. As a last resort, horses which do not respond to any of the methods suggested will have to be turned into hacks. After all, it is just as absurd to try to make a dressage horse out of an animal which is not made correctly to start with.

Refusing to jump, and running out

By 'refusing' we mean that the ridden horse refuses to go over a jump. It will either stop in front of the jump or run out to the side. The competition rule book definition of a refusal does not concern us here. Our purpose is to examine how this form of disobedience – which develops into a bad habit – can be avoided or eliminated. Another matter which is beyond the scope of this study is the question of whether making horses jump outsize fences entails making unnatural demands on them. It has been reliably shown that some horses enjoy jumping, though whether they are always keen to jump big, wide fences, and whether they enjoy doing so over and over again is, to say the least, doubtful. What concerns us here is how to cure a horse of refusing, what are for a horse, normal fences, and to examine why it refuses.

The training of a young horse includes jumping. If no mistakes have been made during this training, we shall have a horse which will jump any normal fence. For one reason or another it can happen that the horse refuses a fence. It is then perhaps handled wrongly, and little by little it is completely ruined, so that it will no longer jump at all or will not do so reliably. There are many reasons why a horse refuses to jump.

One essential observation we can make is that horses with ability, both physical and mental, generally create more problems than those which submit readily to man's will, and 'give in'. Young horses often pose problems during their training. This does not necessarily mean they will turn out to be the worst horses. It can even be said that it is a sign of greater intelligence when a horse resists doing things which do not suit it. In this situation, re-establishing the confidence between horse and rider is particularly important. Not all refusals warrant the description of a bad habit or vice, since in most cases it is the rider who is to blame, for example when he stops giving the aids. It is hard to draw the dividing line, and decide exactly where the fault lies. In this investigation we shall use as a starting point faults which originate in the horse. It is assumed that the horse is not resisting the rider because of some physical defect. Lameness, back pains, shoeing problems, possibly navicular disease, or pain of any kind, can cause a horse to refuse in order to spare itself further pain.

We must look at refusing from a psychological angle. There are some horses which will jump a normal course (i.e. neither hard nor very easy) perfectly once they have jumped the first fence successfully. However, they try to refuse the

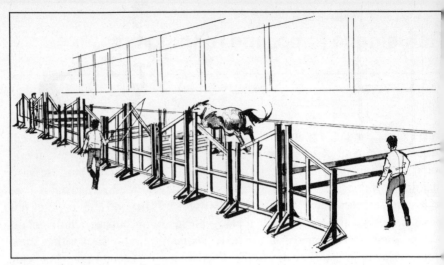

Jumping lane made out of wings.

first jump in order to avoid jumping the whole course. Once the rider ha
succeeded in getting them over the first jump, they will jump the rest of the
course as normal. You also find horses which have an aversion to certain
jumps, and are well aware that after three refusals they can 'go home'. Epi
sodes such as this also show that horses definitely have a memory for numbers
Another example is the horse which has been trained to rein back and ha
always been asked for the same number of steps: if an extra step is asked for i
will hesitate. Maday relates the case of the pit ponies which knew exactly when
they had completed their thirtieth trip of the day and it was time to go back to
the stable.

Another cause of refusing is the colours of the jumps. Horses see colour
differently to us. The horse sees a smaller range of colours than we do, that is
horses can distinguish colours, but they only see a fraction of the colou
spectrum seen by humans. According to Grzimek, horses can recognise the
colours yellow, green, red and blue by their colour quality, but not by their hue
He performed experiments with grey-tinted surfaces of different hues. The
conclusion to be drawn was that a horse obviously sees yellow and green more
clearly than red and blue. Man also sees yellow and green more clearly at a
distance, a fact which has also influenced car paint schemes.

What is for us a brightly coloured show jumping arena with poles, planks
gates, walls and pots of plants of many different colours, looks much les
colourful to a horse. It has been shown that more mistakes are made at jump
made of blue poles than poles of other colours. Hence dark colours (dark red

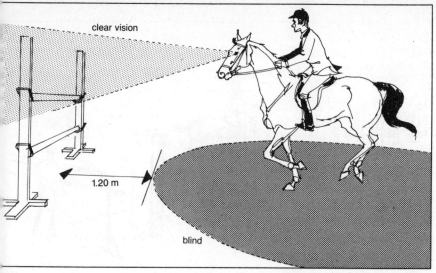

Horse's field of vision before a jump, when the head is raised. The horse cannot see the ground in front of the jump, except the last 1.20 m. (according to SMYTHE).

dark blue) make if more difficult for the horse to discern the jump, while light colours (yellow, green, white) make jumping easier.

Another possible reason for refusal can have its origins in light sensitivity, either to strong light or to sharply contrasting lighting conditions. It is a known fact that fences jumped into the sun are often jumped badly. In evening show jumping competitions the jumps are lit by glaring floodlights, but the areas between the jumps are pools of darkness into which the horse has to jump. It is advisable at these competitions not to stand around in the dark before entering the brightly or glaringly lit arena.

In this connection we must mention another, very important source of problems: the horse's eye. You must have noticed that horses going round a course of jumps often put their heads up or down or to one side before they jump. They are trying to get their eyes in the best position to provide them with a picture of the distance and size of the fence. It is interesting to watch a top class show-jumper ridden between the fences with its chin tucked into its chest, but then given complete freedom of its head just before the jump. Both drawings lead one to conclude that the horse must be given the chance to assess the fence exactly by moving its head.

When horses run out, they tend to do so to the left. This fact should be considered during training, instead of waiting until you are in the arena. Most horses, like people, are 'right-handed', which is reflected by the fact that their manes usually fall on the right. Even in foals it can be seen that horses prefer

87

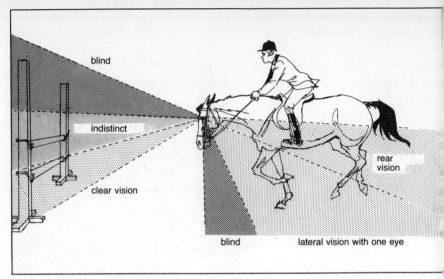

Horse's field of vision before a jump, when the head is lowered (according to SMYTHE).
Note the difference in the field of vision depending on the position of the head.

cantering on the left lead. In early lungeing lessons the horse will keep trying to
spin round when it is on the right rein. Again and again, even during later
training, it will offer its hollow left side.

It is correct to begin by working on the left rein, but as the young horse grows
stronger the right bend should be developed more and more, and the horse
brought onto the right rein. The horse's natural crookedness will continued to
cause problems, especially in advanced dressage training, but Steinbrecht's
famous rule 'Ride your horse forwards and position it straight' should always
apply, and is equally applicable to a horse which is required to jump. What has
been said about right-handed horses is also valid in the case of left-handed
ones, so that every rider should know whether his horse is naturally crooked to
the right or to the left, in order to be able to straighten it. A straight horse
when ridden into a fence with the right leg leading, will also land with this leg
leading.

Any sensitive rider can imagine the strain placed on the horse's tendons and
joints when it lands, for example, on the left leg and then has to make a tight
turn to the right. The horse should be worked in more on the right rein than the
left. Riding-in mainly on the left rein places excessive strain on the right
forefoot and works against straightness. A further piece of advice, by Blen
dinger, is, when you are out hacking and you come to an obstacle which has to
be ridden round and not jumped (e.g. a tree), if you are on a right-footed horse
(i.e. a horse that bends naturally to the left), ride round the right hand side of

88

he obstacle. Continually working at getting the horse used to going round to he right will counteract the tendency to run out to the left. One often finds horses which place their riders to the left in the saddle. This is because the musculature of the withers region is naturally less well developed on the left side. Here again the horse must be worked, especially in collected canter on the right lead, so as to build up the muscles on the left side.

Rearing

A rearing horse has evaded the rider's aids, is refusing to go forwards, and is generally behind the bit. A horse cannot rear while going forwards. In order to rear, it will stop, step back, and then go up. Once a horse has learned that at the first sign of rearing its rider loses confidence, it will use rearing as a means of evading the rider's will. Horses which have a tendency to rear must always be ridden energetically forward. It is also important to make sure that they learn to stand still at the halt. Refusing to stand still develops into rearing with these horses. If it is still possible to keep your weight on the horse's back, sitting into the horse combined with simultaneous powerful (!) use of both spurs can be effective. The horse cannot escape this powerful attack with the spurs while its forehand is off the ground: it must take the punishment. If it leaps forward, on no account must it receive a jab in the mouth, so keep the reins loose! Use of the whip is not very effective – and the horse should definitely not be hit on the head, as is sometimes witnessed.

If the horse does rear, put your legs against it, and make sure your upper body does not go behind the vertical. In fact try to bring it in front of the vertical. The higher the horse rears, the further forwards you should go, so that you are lying on its neck: your weight will influence the horse's balance. You should sit quietly and hold on, with one arm around the horse's neck. The other hand pulls the horse's neck sideways with the rein. Always pull sideways as far as possible, and never backwards. If you pull the neck to the side the horse will not be able to stand straight up because the neck is the balancing pole, so the horse cannot help but come down and put its fore feet back on the ground. If, in the heat of battle, the horse happens to fall over backwards, the rider must quit the stirrups and let himself slide sideways out of the saddle. A horse will never deliberately go over backwards. It does so simply because in the struggle it has lost its balance.

If the horse ends up lying on the ground, there is one drastic and not very attractive course of action which can be taken. This consists of holding the horse's head down on the ground and giving it a few sharp cracks of the whip on its quarters! In a serious and blatant case of disobedience such as this, the punishment must follow immediately, while the horse is lying on the ground, and not when it has got up again. When the punishment does not follow straight away, horses are generally very sensitive to the fact. They recognise the rider's

Rearing horse. The rider on the *left* is sitting correctly, with the upper body leaning forward. He is yielding the reins completely, and so avoiding the risk of the horse falling over backwards. The rider on the *right*, on the other hand, is hanging onto the reins and simply asking for the horse to go over backwards. He is not sitting in the saddle, and his legs are no longer against the horse and so not in a position to react by punishing or driving the horse on with the spur when the moment comes.

uncertainty and his failure to follow a logical sequence. It is also necessary to punish immediately for psychological reasons: the horse does not think 'He's giving me a good hiding because he's cross with me for rearing and falling over backwards'. Rather, it feels 'I've fallen over backwards and had a thrashing, so I won't rear again.'

At the beginning of this chapter the point was made that a rearing horse is evading the rider's forward driving aids, and that the rider should try to send it forward by energetic use of the legs. Therefore, a horse with this vice must be reschooled to respond to the forward driving aids again. In other words, the basic training must be started again from the beginning. The command by the legs to go forwards, which is given hundreds of thousands of times, must become second nature to the horse: it *must* be obeyed. The horse which is answering the leg in a forward, sideways and backward direction, forgets that it can resist, and so loses the desire to do so. The rider's leg does not have physical power over the horse in the way that, for example, a lever type mechanism could. Instead, the influence of the leg is developed into a habit by constantly doing exercises with the horse, and by the horse continuously carrying out commands. Obedience develops, as it were, all by itself.

The horse must also be praised – immediately – every time it obeys a command. The feeling that it is being forced to do something must give way to pleasure derived from the praise and from titbits. If a reward is given every time for achievement, provided it is given immediately, the horse will soon associate achievement with praise. The pleasant experiences associated with the praise (titbits, caressing), serve to invite further achievement.

It is the clever, strong-willed horses which quickly learn that by not going forward they can evade the rider's aids. They stop, and take to rearing: not a very good recommendation for the trainer! It can help to get an assistant to lead the horse by the cheekpiece, or by a lead rein attached to a cavesson. If necessary a second assistant can follow behind with a whip, but he must not hit the horse unless it starts to rear in which case this punishment is backed up by the helper leading the horse forward from the ground. A horse which is laterally flexed, and is going forwards, is unable to rear. By pulling sideways, both rider and helper must prevent the horse straightening or raising its head. If the horse performs a 'lançade' (upward and forward lunge), it must not be jabbed in the mouth. Rather, the forward impulse should be utilised to ride the horse unreservedly forwards. After all the excitement, do not forget the praise. Once the horse has learned its lesson, peace should reign. The horse should enjoy its work. Be generous with the praise and titbits. Usually it is not difficult to get a horse to do something which it will not normally do willingly. It is important, once you have achieved your aim, to take a short break, and give the horse a loose rein, or even dismount and loosen the girths. Best of all, untack and let your horse graze.

Another course of action worth trying is to get another – good – rider to ride the horse. It is possible that with this rider the horse will not rear at all, or will try it once and give up. Sometimes, just thinking about rearing is enough to trigger it off. The thought makes the rider subconsciously tense certain muscle groups. The horse feels this tension and reacts to it accordingly. It is a known fact that horses can perceive the smallest movements and impulses. They can even detect changes in smell (for example sweating due to fear).

Finally, a quote from the famous horseman Fillis: 'Sooner or later in every horse's training there is a struggle. A horse's breaking is not definitely completed if he has made no show of resistance.' And from Le Bon: 'As long as no fight has taken place, the horse cannot be convinced of the rider's superiority.'

Napping

Napping is another way of evading the rider's forward driving aids. The horse will not leave other horses: it 'naps'. Not wanting to leave the stable and refusing to enter the arena are also included in this category, as is, usually, refusing the first jump of a course. Napping is connected with herd instinct, but its cause is not only an excess of herd instinct (every horse has that!). Rather it is caused by 'the fear of anticipated unpleasant experiences' (Blendinger). Moreover, napping can be catching!

When faced with danger, horses bunch together. When a horse is afraid, it runs to the other horses, not away from them. Horses which should not, then, be hit to make them leave the others. Instead, they should be praised for leaving them. Here again the horse must make the association in its mind: 'When I leave the others I get something nice'. It is advisable to do a lot of riding alone, outside as well as in the school. You are better off by yourself than in a ride. If you do have to join a ride, keep changing your position in the ride, ride past it and to the front, turn off from the back of the ride and ride in the opposite direction. A good exercise is to ride out forwards from the ride when it is lined up at the halt. Since there is usually an instructor present with the ride, he or she should lead the napping horse out from the ride to start with. With frequent practise, combined with praise, the horse will gradually give up the habit.

When riding out in company, the nappy horse should be positioned alternately at the front and the back of the ride. Sometimes the ride should go on ahead while the nappy horse remains behind, and sometimes the ride should hang back while it goes on ahead. There are all sorts of possibilities and variations. The rider should select the exercises which will best help the horse to overcome its fear of leaving the 'herd'.

The following scene is commonly witnessed at competitions: a competitor leaves the show-jumping arena. The next rider gets, perhaps, as far as the entrance to the arena, and then stops. i.e. horse and rider proceed to fight it out. The rider wants to go into the arena, the horse refuses obstinately to do so. The groom is on hand and he leads the horse, but it refuses to go any further than the entrance. The horse may not be led in the arena: this would constitute 'outside assistance' according to the competition rules! The horse refuses to allow itself to be backed in either. Sometimes the judges are kind, and make an exception so that the horse may be led in – but this cannot be relied upon. This habit also counts as napping, because the horse is refusing to leave the herd. It is simply afraid of what lies ahead. Sometimes it helps to use the whip – though never to thrash the horse! Napping always involves loss of confidence, so in all cases this needs to be re-established. Another form of the same vice is found in horses which, when out on a ride, refuse to go forwards and escape the rider's control by going backwards. If all else fails, if you are on your own, turn your horse around and go backwards in the direction you wish to go until the horse is tired of it.

To conclude this chapter mention must be made of another bad habit which is only indirectly connected with napping, but is included here because, like napping, it involves clinging – though to the wall and not to other horses. The horse may also try to scrape its rider off. This is a habit which borders on viciousness, and is certainly the result of unpleasant experiences. This is not the

A horse trying to crush its rider against the wall (*left*). The rider should not (attempt to) pull the horse away with the inside rein, since this will only result in his outside leg being squashed even more against the wall (*centre*). Rather, the rider should try to make the horse hollow on the outside (place it in a counter flexion as it were) and obtain obedience with the outside leg (*right*).

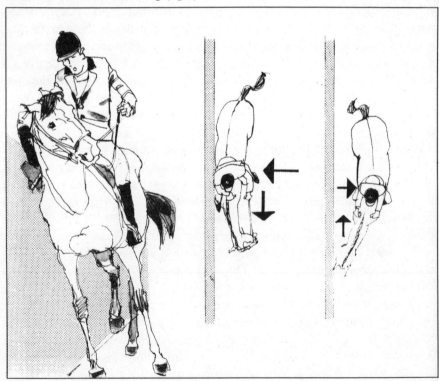

94

place to examine how it has come about, because the causes can be numerous, but what we can do is discuss what needs to be done to remedy the situation once the horse has adopted this practice and tries to scrape the rider off. The horse has managed to escape from the aids, especially the aids of one leg: it evades the action of the leg on the side it rubs against the wall in an attempt to scrape the rider off. We must therefore make the horse obey this leg again. It would be quite wrong to try to pull the horse away from the wall with the opposite rein: this would only serve to make the side which is not obeying the leg even more convex, and enable the horse to press itself and its rider even harder against the wall. We must do the opposite in order to make the side against the wall hollow by bending the horse slightly so that its head is towards the wall, placing more weight on the seat bone of this side (without collapsing the hip!) and moving the horse around its forehand away from the wall.

Bucking

A distinction needs to be made between bucking due to lack of exercise and bucking as a form of resistance. Sigmund Freud recognised that 'the suppression of natural movement can lead to illnesses of a neurotic type, to so-called repression aberrations combined with physical and psychic disturbances'. For the horse, exercise is a primitive, essential element of life, so that for this reason alone the restriction of movement is unnatural. Furthermore, horses have a pronounced urge to play, which is not restricted to youngsters but can also be observed in adult horses in the field, as soon as they have the opportunity to behave in an unrestricted fashion. Every horse-lover has witnessed scenes with horses careering around like mad things, catapulting themselves into the air in truly acrobatic leaps with all four legs vertical, or kicking out to one side, then suddenly farting, taking off and charging away.

So when a horse gives a few high spirited bucks (especially during the first canter of the outing), instead of punishing it, the rider should be pleased that his horse is full of the joys of living. Very often, this type of bucking also occurs at the beginning of a hunt. Other horses may follow suit. Leave room behind you and to the sides to ensure the person riding beside or behind you does not get kicked. Grip with your knees, but without clinging on with your lower leg or (even worse) tickling the horse with the spurs and inciting it to further bucking. When the bucking occurs in canter, that is, in forward movement, for a normal, trained rider there are no grounds for panic. In fact quite the reverse should be the case: he should take pleasure in the horse's desire to go forward. After a few bucks the horse will have let off steam and will canter on quietly. Clamp your knees on and sit these bucks out by adopting a 'jumping seat', with the seat out of the saddle, the upper body inclined forward slightly, and your hands supported on the horse's neck. If this high spirited behaviour gets out of hand it is permissible to check the horse calmly but sharply with one hand in an upward (never a downward) direction. You can also calm the horse by use of the voice, or even shout at it. 'Stop it!' said in a loud voice can be a good substitute for the use of the whip or checking the horse with the hand.

Horses have a pronounced desire to imitate, which accounts for the fact that bucking can be 'catching'. Every rider knows how quick horses are to respond to the trumpet call (a loud emission of wind!) of one of their fellows by indulging in a communal bucking session. You could almost be forgiven for thinking that the horses' faces assume a satisfied expression if one or more riders falls off and they can have a breather.

Bucking as a form of resistance is a different matter. The causes will be discussed later, but first we shall deal with the action to be taken when a horse bucks. In contrast to the horse which bucks in canter, the horse which bucks from resistance is evading the forward driving aids. The same criteria are involved as in rearing. Try to get the horse to go forwards. A sharp stroke of the whip at the first sign of bucking is often helpful. Get your horse going forward from the leg and keep it there. Lean the upper body back slightly, keep your seat in the saddle and sit out the bucks. It would be quite wrong to lean forwards, because in all probability you would be pitched over the horse's head. Do not hold on by the reins! It is no disgrace to hold on to the pommel to enable you to keep your seat in the saddle. You can also hold on to a strap attached to the front of the saddle or to a handful of mane. Obviously you must not throw the reins away: you must make sure that the horse does not put its head between its legs, because if it does you will have no control at all. With its head raised or pulled to the side, a horse can neither buck nor hump its back, especially if it is also ridden energetically forwards. You are at an advantage if you are prepared when the horse first tries to buck. When it does so, close your

It is certainly no disgrace to hold on to the front of the saddle on a bucking horse. In this way you can pull yourself down into the saddle (*left*). The rider on the *right* will most probably be catapulted over the horse's head at the next buck.

knees against the saddle, check sharply in an upward direction, use your whip on its shoulder to prevent it lashing out (which is part of bucking), and perhaps shout at it. Doing all these things simultaneously and quickly can prevent further bucking.

However nice it is to ride a horse with a bit of life in it, bucking out of high spirits should not be allowed to develop into a habit. If the first stride of canter on springy ground is used as an excuse for a bit of fun, and to let off steam, the above measures should be adopted from the outset. A tap on the shoulder, a gentle check (the severity depends on how sensitive the horse is), and the horse will behave itself. With some horses, bucking quickly becomes a habit if they are not made to understand from the outset that it is unacceptable. Many horses will keep 'trying it on' with a weak rider, and will set about it in earnest once they have succeeded in dislodging their rider.

The causes of bucking may have their origins in pain. Horses which tense when saddled may buck to try to escape from the restriction of the saddle. Ways of coping with this have already been described; to these I can only add that such horses must be handled carefully – punishment is inappropriate. Lungeing the horse with the girth only partially tightened is one good way to deal with this. Walking the horse for a while with the girth not fully tightened has been

The horse will be prevented from bucking if the rider can only raise its head.

shown to be effective. The horse should be given as much freedom of its head as possible so that it does not feel restricted. Trotting should not be attempted until the girth has been (gradually) tightened up.

While on this subject, the deliberately provoked bucking of the rodeo bronco is worthy of mention. These horses are made to buck by tightening a strap around the belly behind the rib-cage. At best this strap is uncomfortable for the horse; at worst it causes pain. As soon as the strap is loosened the horse stops bucking. In my opinion, this must surely verge on an infringement of the animal cruelty law.

Some horses are extraordinarily sensitive in their backs, and the slightest movement will make them at least kick out with their hind legs. Clothing touching the back is one thing which can trigger off bucking. The remedy for this is self-evident. If there is nothing touching the horse, the saddle lining and numnah should be closely examined. There may also be something wrong with the horse's back underneath the saddle, such as a sore or abscess caused by an ill-fitting saddle or numnah, by faults in the saddle lining, by friction from a numnah stiff with sweat or by twisted, pinching girths etc. A good rider will, as a matter of course, check the horse's back, as well as its legs, for injury after every ride. Ill-fitting saddles, which press and rub under the seat as well as at the withers, are quite common causes of misbehaviour in the ridden horse.

You also find horses which are extraordinarily ticklish under their bellies. With these horses, cantering in snow, for example can result in spectacular bucks when lumps of snow are thrown up and hit them under the belly. Punishment is pointless in such cases, because it does not eliminate the ticklishness, which the horse cannot help.

Wind-suckers and crib-biters sometimes show a tendency to buck when the wind which has built up inside them is causing them problems. They should be ridden as far as possible on straight lines, i.e. not on small circles or voltes, and not flexed.

Sexual irregularities can also lead to resisistance. Cryptorchids ('rigs') often become sly, nasty and extremely aggressive as a result of their rudimentary sexual development. The most logical solution in such cases is surgery, the more so since exaggerated stallion behaviour in the stable as well as among other horses leads to all sorts of problems.

Nymphomaniac mares, which are often extremely irritable because they are in a state of permanent sexual excitement, can also be a source of problems. They are ticklish as well as unpredictable, and their unpredictability means that they cannot be, or are not amenable to, being worked or handled in any logical fashion. Here again the veterinary surgeon should be consulted because, as with cryptorchids, an operation is possible (ovariectomy). This abnormal excitability must be distinguished from the symptoms of normal oestrus, which are well known. The behaviour of a mare in oestrus, like that of the abnormal mare, may be characterised by nervous excitement, frequent whinnying, restlessness, capricious appetite, increased water intake, irritability, over-activity and ticklishness. However, the reverse may be the case, i.e. the mare may be apathetic, stubborn and resistant. Symptoms vary with the individual, and it is possible to 'work around them' because they can be predicted and are of limited duration. Apart from the fact that a little consideration is required, normal mares present little problem.

Pulling, running away

I should like to start this chapter by quoting a rider whose horses were always sensitively ridden, on a very light rein, and never pulled. The rider in question, General the Count Pejachevich, had only one arm. He was an excellent rider, and was once asked how it was that his horses never pulled. His answer was as concise as it was subtle: 'Because I cannot hold them!' A rider with heavy hands will receive the whole of the weight of the horse's head and neck in his hands. Light hands, on the other hand, meet only with mild opposition.

A horse is said to be 'pulling' when it seeks a 'fifth foot' in the rider's hand while cantering or galloping out on a ride. It leans hard on the bit, often as the result of a keen temperament, strong use of the hands by the rider, or weak hindquarters. This is an unpleasant habit, especially in the hunting field.

Correct training is the only way the rider can be sure that his horse will not pull. Even moving off while the rider is mounting is a form of running away, because the horse which is allowed to get away with this will not have the slightest respect for the restraining action of the rider's hand in canter. If the rider does not even know how to control his horse while he is getting on, he will certainly not be able to do so once the horse is in movement.

With horses with difficult temperaments, pulling can be quite a problem. It is interesting that such horses will sometimes pull with one rider and not with another. However hard it seems, if the fault is due to the horse having too difficult a temperament for its rider, then the rider should get rid of it.

Frequent references have been made throughout this book to correct training in connection with behaviour problems. It is beyond the book's scope to go into the fundamental rules of the (as far as possible) ideal training of the horse, and indeed of the rider. A few important points, however, do need to be made. We will assume that the horse in question does not have any serious conformation defects which make it physically very difficult for it to balance itself in the required way. The first, important, point is that it is quite pointless to put more and more severe bits on a horse which is heavy in hand and tends to pull. This will only make matters worse. The sharper the bit, the duller the horse's mouth will become. The less sensitive the horse's mouth becomes, the less it will help to fit the most severe curb, with the longest cheeks, the biggest port and the tightest curb-chain. The horse finishes up with a 'dead mouth'. Even the most hideous injuries inflicted on the horse will not prevent it taking hold of the bit

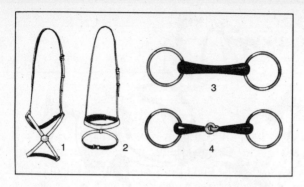

1. Grackle noseband
2. Flash noseband
3. Rubber snaffle
4. Jointed rubber snaffle

and, finally, running away, which is an extreme form of pulling. Horses with sensitive mouths sometimes discover that the best way to escape from the pain inflicted by the rider's hand is to take hold of the bit in their teeth, hang on to it, and so take control.

To stay with the subject of bits, use a thick snaffle, or even a rubber snaffle (jointed, not a straight bar). Fit it slightly higher in the horse's mouth than usual. Try out various types of mild bits. There have been cases of horses which have not responded to any kind of bit, but for whom a hackamore turned out to be a good solution. A hackamore is something completely different, but it is worth a try. It is also worth checking that the drop noseband is not too low, and so pressing on the nostrils and restricting the breathing. Having its breathing cut off can make a horse panic and can be done very easily by compressing the soft, sensitive pieces of cartilage in the nose. If this is the case, it is worth trying a cavesson noseband or, if necessary, a flash noseband. Flash nosebands restrict the breathing less, and yet make it more difficult for the horse to open its mouth and so escape the restraining rein aids. The grackle noseband serves a similar purpose.

If the horse runs away, it is fundamentally wrong to lean back, put the legs forward, brace them in the stirrups and pull on the reins. If the horse cannot be prevented from running away by strong use of the reins, and this has only served to increase the tension between horse and rider, you must have the courage to drive the horse even more forwards, possibly by energetic use of the spurs (with an almost loose rein, of course). The aim is to get the horse back on the aids. Raising the horse's head very high, combined with energetic use of the seat and legs ('sitting into the horse'), can serve both to prevent the horse 'taking off' and to bring it back onto the aids. Another possibility is to turn the horse's head to one side and bring it first onto a large circle, and then decrease the size of the circle until you can bring the horse to a halt. The hand which is asking for the flexion (usually the left) should be as low as possible. The other hand should hold the rein as short as possible and should be supported on the

102

The rider on the *left* is riding a runaway horse with his feet braced against the stirrups, which is incorrect. He is pulling with his hands too high and the horse's martingale too short, instead of trying to stop the horse from pulling. The rider on the *right*, on the other hand, is making his horse yield by correct riding, in a 'jumping seat' with his legs against the horse and his hands low.

neck. Most horses are naturally crooked: they tend to have a false right bend, and, consequently they usually lie on the left rein and are unwilling to accept the right rein. We take advantage of the hollow 'flexion' of the left side to turn the horse to the side which it 'offers'. Most horses are born right-footed, i.e. they are naturally bent to the left. Except in exceptional cases, the right side is stiffer.

A horse which 'takes off' in a panic usually does so with its head in the air and its back hollow. Hence the rider should try to lower the head. Except in the extreme case described above (the panicking horse), it can be helpful to hold the hands at the same level as the horse's mouth in keeping with the well-known rule: the higher the horse's head, the higher the rider's hand, and the lower the

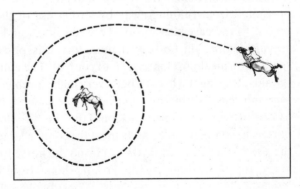

A horse which goes out of control while out on a ride should be ridden on a spiral shaped track to bring it to a halt.

horse's head, the lower the hand. You can also try lowering the bit in the horse's mouth.

Horses with conformation defects, such as low set-on ewe necks, weak backs and sway backs are particularly prone to this form of running away. In the other form the horse leans on the hand and 'takes off' with its head down, having caught hold of the bit in its teeth. This is dealt with by carrying the hands low and giving a sharp upward pull, or by steering the horse to one side as described above.

Apart from actually correcting the bad habit, the rider should undertake the following retraining exercises: working canter in a large field, first on a normal circle, and then gradually increasing the size of the circle; do the same exercise on both reins. Increase the speed to a medium and extended canter, and then go back to a working canter. Work all the time in a 'jumping seat'. Calm the horse by talking to it frequently, and praising and patting it. The horse must be able to remain decontracted while working at speed, and not 'hot up'. The rider's hands should rest on the horse's crest and remain perfectly still, exerting only the minimum of pressure in the half-halts and the decreases of tempo. On no account must the hands move backward, and under no circumstances must the horse be allowed to assume a faster tempo than you have asked for.

A calming effect is also obtained by making a 'bridge' on the withers with the reins: the left rein is crossed over the withers to the right side, and the right rein to the left side, so that the reins are held in the normal position, but each hand

Cantering in a 'jumping seat' with the small of the back 'tightened' slightly relieves the horse's back of weight and allows it to swing. The hands lie on the crest and have a 'yielding tendency'. The lower legs should lie lightly but positively against the horse's sides. The canter strides should cover plenty of ground. A horse which is pulled together from the front and not ridden from behind will not be capable of covering the ground.

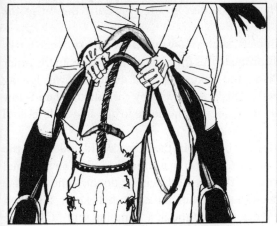
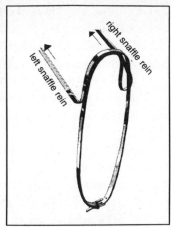

Making a 'bridge' is a good way of keeping the rider's hands steady and at the same time giving him some security. Moreover, the feeling of the hands against the sides of the withers has a calming effect on the horse.

holds both reins. This ensures that the hands (which are both held at the same height) have a steady, firm grip, and that the action of the reins is 'quiet', and not backward. Both hands yield along the horse's crest in the direction of the horse's mouth as soon as the rider feels that the horse is beginning to yield to the bit. Also, make sure you use the correct aids and get your horse used to the idea that the restraining aids do not come only from the hands, but that a slightly drawn back leg has a 'guarding' effect.

The leg, resting against the horse's side without 'gripping up', plays an important role in regulating the tempo, and the horse must learn to respect it. When you come to a field where you intend to canter, do not simply go charging off. Do not go too fast, even if all around you other horses and riders are making their getaway. Even try to stay in walk or trot, and if possible canter in the direction of a wood, so that there is something in front of the horse to stop it, and not just a wide open space. It is also important to canter only for short periods, so that the horse does not have a chance to build up speed. The whole thing must be treated as a schooling session. On no account must the horse be allowed to exceed the normal contact and lean on the bit. Any tendency to do so must be immediately nipped in the bud.

In the hunting field it is not unusual to see despairing riders battling to regain control of horses which are running away as if in panic. Young and inexperienced horses must be accustomed systematically to hunting. A hack, accustomed only to going along the same, familiar routes at a nice, easy canter, can suddenly lose its head and go out of control (quite inexplicably as far as the rider is concerned) when it finds itself among lots of unknown horses in a large

A pulling horse cannot be brought back under control if the rider's legs are nowhere near the horse's sides (*above*). The rider in the bottom picture has adopted a 'jumping seat' and lowered his hands, and so has more chance of getting his horse back 'on the aids'.

hunt. Moreover, horses are not usually allowed to exert themselves prior to a hunt, so that they save their strength for the big occasion. This is a completely wrong point of view if the horse is of the type which tries to release its pent-up energy during the hunt by engaging in one long, pointless battle, which serves only to exhaust its rider. If a horse is to go hunting, preparation is needed. It is more sensible to start giving the horse a work-out several days beforehand (not counting fitness training), and it is not as ridiculous as it may seem, on the day of the hunt to give the horse a certain amount of work in the morning, prior to hunting in the afternoon. Provided the necessary care is taken, there is not even anything wrong with covering long distances twice in one day in calm and harmony. Battling with the rider puts a far greater strain on the horse than this.

Jogging

Horses which jog are sheer misery – both for the rider and for themselves. The rider cannot leave the horse alone, and horse and rider are worn out by the constant dancing around and usually unsuccessful attempts to make the horse walk. After a while the rider gives up, and lets the horse keep on jogging. The more it jogs, the more restless it becomes. It begins to sweat, wastes its energy, and places undue strain on its tendons and joints. With a few exceptions, the cause of jogging is usually to be found in the fact that the horse is evading the aids and is not in balance. The rider is often to blame. If a rider knows how to put his horse correctly 'on the aids', his horse will not start jogging, and if he is a good rider he will be able to bring a jogging horse back to walk.

If the cause of jogging lies in the horse's temperament, the habit is more difficult to correct. Here too, however, a change of rider may be the answer, since an aversion to a particular rider can make a horse restless. Calming words often help, and holding both reins in one hand and resting the other on the horse's neck is sometimes successful. It is advisable not to ride at the back of a group of horses and riders. Ride a few horse's lengths in front instead. It is often effective to ride away in the opposite direction to the group, or to ride alongside it. Another horse in the group may have a particular affection for your horse, and have a calming effect on it. If so, ride along with it.

The one thing you must not do is allow the horse to continue jogging. Sitting down in the saddle, with the lower leg lightly against the horse, and the back and seat fully 'engaged' to drive the horse forwards, are basic essential conditions for putting the horse back on the aids when it has managed to get behind the bit and is not obeying the driving action of the legs. It is fundamentally wrong to sit forward and stick the legs out, away from the horse, so that you have no influence over it. It takes a lot of patience to settle a confirmed jogger so that it will walk on a long rein again. There is always a way, however. Leg-yielding to the point of desperation is one possibility. No horse can jog while it is doing this exercise, but it must be performed correctly, with the horse correctly on the bit, i.e. neither above nor behind the bit and with a steady contact. Then ride for a long period in shoulder-in (do both these exercises on both reins). Do not stop until you feel you can ride straight ahead again. The hind legs must be made to take long, ground-covering strides again, instead of little half-steps.

(*Left*): The wrong way to sit on a jogging horse. (*Right*): correct seat, hands on the withers calming the horse.

The other riders in the group must co-operate with your retraining programme, and not just 'do their own thing'. Get off the horse from time to time and lead it, since this can have a calming effect. Let it graze, and during retraining avoid hunts and other activities which could cause it to become excited. You should also check the fitting and the condition of the tack. A pinching bit or saddle, a rubbing girth or a drop noseband fitted too low can unsettle a horse. If your horse jogs on the way back to the stable, turn round, go home if possible by another route, halt, dismount and stand with the horse for as long as it takes for it to calm down. This is an appropriate point to mention that eliminating behaviour problems, vices and bad habits takes time – and sometimes a great deal of time. On no account must the rider become impatient.

Stumbling

There is a basic distinction to be made between the stumbling of young horses and the stumbling of older horses. With young horses, stumbling can be caused by loss of balance, or the horse not having yet found its balance under the rider, as well as by serious defects in conformation. It must therefore be given exercises which develop its feeling for balance and enable it to balance itself under the rider's weight. Work over poles on the ground and cavalletti, and riding up hills and on uneven and yielding ground, especially in woods, is very good for hardening and strengthening the young horse's tendons and ligaments. It is important that it learns to lower its head and look where it is going, and so become sure-footed. When, as a result of these exercises, the horse becomes stronger and generally more developed, especially in its back muscles, it will stop stumbling.

With older horses, stumbling can have various causes. Here again the reason may be conformation defects, such as upright pasterns or a straight shoulder. However, the horse may be on the forehand, and have been ridden by a rider who has allowed it to lean permanently on the bit, so that the bit has become a 'fifth foot' for it. The cause may also lie in weakness or lack of energy, possibly made worse by overtiredness at the end of a long ride. Shoeing is another possible cause. Ask your blacksmith, as it may just be that the feet are too long, or he may adjust the shape of the shoe at the toe. Once all these possibilities have been eliminated, it only remains for the rider to bring the horse off its forehand, to re-establish its balance. This entails starting basic training again from the beginning. The back muscles must be strengthened so that the hind legs are encouraged to step further under the body again. The horse must relearn that it cannot simply shuffle along, but must carry itself – and its rider.

In the days of cavalry, on long marches the sergeant, who rode at the back of the squadron, would note down in his little book the names of all the horses which stumbled and dawdled along with their riders asleep on their backs. This was not completely fair, however, since there are some horses which are naturally predisposed to stumbling.

It is important to understand that a horse which is 'on the aids' will either not stumble at all, or will stumble less. If a horse is stumbling through tiredness, the only thing to do is get off and either lead it or take a rest.

In many cases, as has been mentioned, the horse's feet need to be examined and treated. Horses with very hard, dry feet are particularly prone to stumbling. There is an English saying: 'No foot, no horse', which means that if a horse's legs are not in order it is no good (for riding). Horses which stumble can be the cause of some very unpleasant experiences for the rider, as well as a source of danger to themselves (damaged knees and fetlocks).

While on this subject, mention should be made of horses which have had a neurectomy to relieve the pain of navicular disease, and for this reason have lost all sensation in their feet. Such horses can pose problems when riding across country – and also in the jumping arena – because they no longer have any feeling in their feet. The horse's sure-footedness must necessarily be affected for the worse if the nerves which play an essential part in it are severed.

Dragging the toes

Sometimes one sees horses dragging the toe of one or both hind feet on the floor of the school. This is most common in walk, but can also occur in trot. Riding school horses, which have a different rider on their back every lesson and have become stultified by riding school life, tend to shuffle away their hours in the school with stiff hind legs and their toes dragging wearily on the ground. However, even horses with essentially very active hindquarters can suddenly drag a toe across the ground. This can even happen at the beginning of the lesson, and is certainly not due to tiredness. It is more a question of laziness, and the only way to combat it is through active use of the driving aids. In walk, on flat ground, the horse should put its hind feet down as far forward as possible under its body, and not drag them lazily across the ground. Frequent work over grids of poles on the ground spaced at walk distances (0.8 to 1 m) will develop the activity of the hindquarters. As a progression from this, cavalletti about 15 to 20 cm high can be used, and the horse worked over these in medium trot.

As we know, in medium walk the horse should tread with its hind feet beyond the prints of its fore feet. Apart from developing the ground covering capacity, the above exercises also activate the quarters and develop the rhythm, especially with horses which do not have a good walk rhythm. The rider should first bring his horse onto the bit, i.e. establish a soft contact between his hand (which should be kept still) and the horse's mouth by pushing carefully with his back and legs. The cavalletti or poles on the ground should be approached straight, and just before the horse reaches them the rider should drop his hands as low as possible, and by moving them forwards in the direction of the horse's mouth, allow it to stretch its neck downwards. The rider follows this movement, leaning his upper body forward, therefore taking his weight off the horse's back so that it can move without tension. It is very important that the rider uses his driving aids, and rides the horse straight and forwards. A horse which is being ridden forwards will pick its feet up energetically. The contact with the mouth should be maintained, but the horse should not be prevented from swinging its back by a high or rigid hand. It must be taught to move with its back, and not just with its legs.

Increasing the distance between the poles will make the horse take longer, more ground-covering strides, and raising the height of the cavalletti will benefit the collection in the collected walk. The work over cavalletti can lead on to the next stage of training if the rider has the knowledge to build on the success obtained in the early work. The same principles apply to the work in trot as to the walk, though the distances between poles is increased to 1.3 m. The distance from the middle of one cavalletti to the middle of the next can be measured by placing one foot in front of the other: it should come to about five foot-lengths. It is beyond the scope of this book to go into the specifications and the method for trot work aimed at increasing collection.

Mention should be made, however, of working in hand to increase collection. This is an excellent way to teach the horse to increase the activity of its hindquarters. It should be carried out first without a rider. The horse is saddled and bridled (in a snaffle) and positioned on the outside track on the long side of the school. The horse is either controlled by a cavesson, and wears side reins on both sides, or it has a side rein only on the opposite side to that on which the trainer is standing. The trainer stands facing the hindquarters, level with the horse's shoulder. When working on the left rein, the reins are held in the left hand and the whip in the right. For work on the right rein the positions are reversed. The whip is positioned along the horse's body. The horse can also be worked without side reins by the following method: the reins are unbuckled in

Position of the trainer, and of his hands, during work in hand.

the middle and the outside rein is passed over the horse's neck about two hands' breadth behind the ears and threaded through the inside snaffle ring from inside to out. Both reins are held in the left hand (when on the left rein), close to the bit. When checking the horse, the hands act in an upward direction. The trainer, walking backwards, leads the horse forward with a light hand. The whip, the voice, and clicking with the tongue are used to send the horse on. It should take short ('half') steps. Do only a little at a time and do not ask for too much to start with. Do not forget to praise the horse when it has worked willingly. Keep taking short breaks, since the horse should not be tense for this work. Once the horse has understood what it is supposed to be doing, it will go willingly into the hand. Then you can start working the horse from the saddle with an assistant giving the whip aids. Here too it is important that the horse is ridden with a light hand. On no account must collection cause the horse to have a hard contact. It is also important to keep the horse straight. On no account must it turn its hindquarters into the school or move them outwards, by going against the whip or leg. This fault is particularly common in work on the left rein. It should be counteracted by turning off the track onto a volte, returning to the track in a shoulder-in, and then working for a while with a slight inward flexion (inside 'position').

Tongue faults, noisy mouth, gnashing the teeth, opening the mouth, head tossing

This section is a very complex and difficult one. As a general rule, however, it can be said that the rider is to blame for most bad habits involving the tongue. Horses will find all sorts of ways to counteract the incorrect and at the same time often very painful actions of an unskilful or hard hand. They may put the tongue over the bit, or stick it out of the side of the mouth. They also know how to conceal the fact that they have done so, so that their unskilled riders often fail to realise (or at least not straight away), that their horse is not correctly on the bit. Contact with the bit depends on temperament and conformation. Horses with weak hindquarters, which push more than carry, often have a stronger contact because they are permanently 'running on'. If the rider is not in a position to stop the running through correct riding, the contact will become stronger and stronger. 'Running on' can also result from stiff hindquarters. The horse's mouth becomes harder as a result of this practice, until finally it is completely 'dead', i.e. impervious to the action of the reins. It is an almost impossible undertaking to restore sensitivity to the horse's mouth once this has happened.

Some horses will try to counteract the constant 'strap hanging', hammering, and rough action of uncontrolled hands by twisting and turning their tongues. Bad habits involving the tongue can also be caused by ill-fitting bits. Particularly in the early stages of riding young horses, care must be taken to ensure that the bit is neither too narrow nor too wide. There should be one centimetre protruding from the mouth on either side. The joint of the bit should not be worn, have sharp edges, or pinch. It is a well-known fact that the thinner the bit, the more severe it is. With curb bits, particular care should be taken with fitting.

The height of the snaffle in the mouth should be such that the lips are not drawn upwards. A snaffle fitted too low will encourage a young horse to play with the unfamiliar object in its mouth. It will try to spit it out or to push it forward with the tongue.

If the bit is too low in the mouth and the young horse has a very mobile tongue (very fleshy tongues are less mobile), it may get its tongue over the top of the bit. This is one way that tongue problems start. The horse will try again and again to get rid of the annoying object in its mouth. So from the outset you should fit the bit too high rather than too low. Once the horse has come to terms with the bit, and has confidence in the rider's hand, it is unlikely to adopt this habit.

A jointed rubber snaffle is also worth trying. Although with young horses special care should be taken not to fit the bit too high, and therefore too tight in the mouth, it should be somewhat higher than usual so as to restrict the mobility of the tongue. An even better solution can be a flash noseband. It restricts the breathing less than a drop noseband and makes it more difficult for the horse to open its mouth and get its tongue over the bit.

Sometimes tongue problems are the result of pain in the quarters or hind legs. In nervous horses they can also be caused by excitement. On no account should early signs of bad habits involving the tongue be brushed to one side. The first signs serve as a warning, they are the horse's way of telling you that it is not happy with the way it is being treated, or even that it is in pain. If you notice that your horse has its tongue over the bit, if you have no assistant you must dismount and remedy the situation before continuing your work. One solution is a snaffle with a double, spoon-shaped tongue grid. The 'spoons' lying on the tongue should prevent the horse getting its tongue over the top of the bit.

You can also try weaving a number of tail hairs into the joint of the bit and then chopping the ends off so that the cut ends tickle the tongue and palate. You can also get bits which have several, small chain links built into the joint for the purpose of making the horse's mouth more mobile. Bits with 'mouthing chains' work in the same way. You can improvise one of these by using a curb chain. Double-jointed snaffles (French snaffles) and snaffles with a double

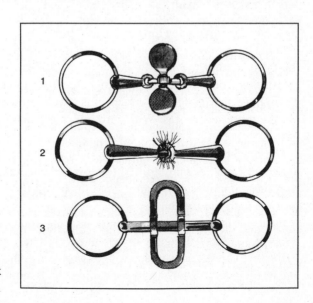

1. Bit with spoon-shaped double tongue grid.
2. Snaffle with horse hairs woven into the joint.
3. Bit for horses which stick their tongues out.

115

mouthpiece have a similar action. There is no hard and fast rule for curing tongue problems once they have occurred. As has already been said, it is usually the rider who is to blame: they do not occur spontaneously.

Bad habits involving the tongue must not simply be ignored by the rider, because the more difficult the schooling exercises become, the more the horse will evade the bit's action by twisting its tongue about. Look out for this problem when buying a horse. A horse, even a young one, which puts its tongue over the bit or lets it hang out of the side of the mouth will be a constant source of problems, even for a good rider. Usually the tongue hangs out on the side the horse leans on the bit. Often it does not actually hang out in full view, but is inserted like a cushion between the bit and the bar of the mouth to soften the action of the bit. In this position it is less noticeable. One possible cure lies in temporarily taking a stronger contact on this rein, and at the same time applying the leg on the same side more strongly. The hand then yields immediately. The horse must be praised straight away if this method succeeds. This fault will take time and patience to cure. The rider should keep reminding himself that it is he and his wrong handling which are to blame, and consequently he is the one who can put matters right. With patience and more patience, and through a quiet, sensitive hand, supported by a supple seat, he must reschool his horse from this bad and unpleasant habit. Tying the tongue down with a strap or cord is no answer, even if this method has been, or is still, used by certain well-known riders.

It is also interesting to note that the snaffle normally acts on the tongue and the edges of the lower lip which cover the bars, and not on the tongue and the bars themselves. An unsteady, hard hand can cause the thin edges of the lips to be pushed back, exposing the bars, and can also exert painful pressure. Since the tongue is the most sensitive part of the mouth, the horse escapes the pain by sticking its tongue out.

Horses may also squeeze their tongue out between their incisor teeth, a habit which may not be immediately noticed by the rider. This can be dealt with by judiciously tightening the (drop) noseband.

An unpleasant habit adopted by some horses is gnashing or grinding the teeth. However, a distinction must be made between violent, angry gnashing, usually with laid back ears and accompanied from time to time by opening of the mouth, and a quieter version performed with a closed, wet mouth. The first kind is always a serious fault, and shows that the contact is not steady and the horse is not in harmony with its rider. Horses which do this are not free from constraint: they are physically and mentally tense. On the other hand, the even, rhythmical, grinding with the mouth closed gives more an impression of well-being. It is certainly an aesthetic blemish, but the horses concerned have a good contact and are in harmony with their riders.

116

Horses which mouth and rattle their bits are not completely free from constraint. They do not have an even contact, and are avoiding paying attention to the rider. This fault is a sign of incorrect training. However, there are two kinds of mouthing the bit: a noisy rattling with open mouth, and a soft 'clink' with closed mouth. Seunig states: 'In contrast to the noisy gnashing and clattering which coincide with the rhythm of the gait, the soft "clink" of the bit is not a fault but quite the reverse: it is welcome music to the rider's ear. It takes the form of an almost inaudible, non-rhythmic "clink", produced by the tongue falling back into its channel, after the swallowing action resulting from correct mouthing, and allowing the two bits it has lifted to drop back into place, with the mouthpiece of the bridoon clinking against that of the curb as they do so.'

Tongue problems can occur during the transition from snaffle to double bridle. The extra bit in its mouth can cause the horse to open its mouth or play with the bits with its tongue. Problems can also be caused by inexperienced riders handling the reins, and especially when the horse is ridden more on the curb than the bridoon. It is important for the hand to be light and not to have a pulling action. Holding the reins in the 3:1 position (i.e. right snaffle rein in the right hand, the other reins in the left) is beneficial, because the right hand can make adjustments more easily. It must not be forgotten that with the reins in the 3:1 position the left hand must be held in front of the middle of the rider's stomach, otherwise the right curb rein is overtightened!

Now for the promised remarks about the correct position and adjustment of a double bridle. First of all the choice of curb is important, since riding with a curb is a big change from what the horse is used to. A thin mouthpiece is more severe than a thick one, especially if the horse does not have very fleshy bars. The higher the port, the more severe the bit's action. The port also serves to accommodate the tongue and give it freedom to move. Horses with thick, fat tongues should therefore be fitted with a bit which leaves plenty of space for the tongue. The width of the bit must also be correct. If the mouthpiece is too narrow, the cheeks of the bit press against the lips and cause discomfort and pain. If it is too wide it will not remain still in the horse's mouth, but will be pulled backwards and forwards through the mouth. Moreover, the curb chain will also move about. The proportions of the upper and lower cheeks, and the length of the upper cheek in relation to the lower should also be considered, because the shorter the upper cheek and the longer the lower cheek, the stronger is the lever action. Likewise, the less the difference in length between the upper and lower cheeks, the milder the curb's action. The lower cheek is normally twice the length of the upper cheek. The position of the curb chain must also be checked carefully. It is hooked first onto the right hand hook, and then turned to the right (i.e. twisted round) until it lies flat and evenly in the curb groove. With horses whose curb grooves are only thinly covered with flesh, a rubber or leather curb guard may help. If possible the chain should be made up of broad, flat links. The ring in the middle is for the so-called 'lip strap' to pass through, and should always be on the outside of the chain. The lip strap is for use on curbs with straight cheeks, when the horse is in the habit of 'snatching' at the cheeks with its teeth. Another way of preventing this habit is to use a curb with 'S' shaped cheeks (show-hack bit). These bits are no longer very popular.

The curb chain makes the lever action possible. It also limits it (to forty-five degrees from the line of the mouth). Too much play in the cheek (where it makes an angle of more than forty-five degrees) is less of a fault than not enough play (less than forty-five degrees), and can even be recommended for early training in the double bridle.

Particular care should be taken that the curb fits in all respects because faults can develop which, once they have become habits, are very difficult to cure.

Flapping, or smacking, the lips is a subject about which there is little to say, except that it is practically incurable. One reason for the horse developing this habit is too much sugar. The horse does not like the sticky feeling in its mouth, and starts flapping its sticky lips against each other. If you do give your horse a little reward, it is always better to give either pieces of apple – not too large or the horse will have difficulty eating them with its bit in its mouth – or even bits of bread, which has the advantage that it takes on the smell of the rider's hand. Apple slices assist the production of foam in the horse's mouth, but the foam

(*Left*): Positions of the cheek of the curb. 1: The bit 'cannot move': adjustment is too severe. 2: Correct position: cheek at forty-five degrees. 3: Too much play in the cheek: the bit is almost completely ineffective.
(*Right*): The correct position of curb and bridoon on the lower jaw.

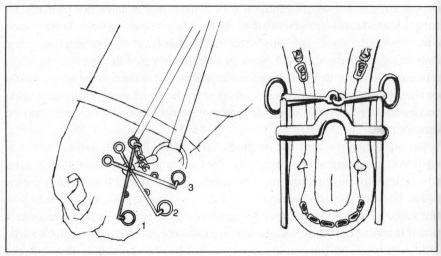

they produce is not sticky. Little cubes containing vitamins, minerals, sugar and fillers are now available as a substitute for sugar. Many horses will not eat them at first, but they gradually get used to them. Incidentally, the foam produced by eating sugar is a very bright white, while 'natural' foam is not.

Two more bad habits which fall into the same category are opening the mouth and shaking the head. Both are, to a greater or lesser extent, the result of incorrect training. One way for a horse to evade the action of a hard hand is to open its mouth wide, and it will do so especially if it has not learnt to flex at the poll. A non-elastic hand is usually the starting point of the trouble. The liaison between the driving and the restraining aids is broken, and often the horse is also stiff in its quarters and rigid in its back. The best way to combat this is by reviewing and developing the horse's suppleness, *Durchlässigkeit*, and by performing lots of transitions from one gait to another. Particularly recommended are flowing transitions from canter to trot and transitions from trot to walk and straight back to trot. The reins are held elastically, with the joints of the hands absorbing the movement. If the horse sets itself against one rein, the rein is immediately 'shaken' (vibrated). Transitions from working trot to medium trot and vice versa are also good, as are the same exercises in canter – particularly on a circle, and with frequent changes of rein. If opening the mouth is not accompanied by other symptoms, tightening the drop noseband will help. A flash noseband is particularly recommended because it does not make it so easy for the horse to open its mouth.

Head-shaking is usually the outward sign of discomfort due to the hands acting too strongly. One course of action is to fit a running martingale or a (German) standing martingale (this consists of a strap running from the girth to a coupling attached to the bit rings, usually with rubber insert, and with no neckstrap), but it does not get to the root of the problem and it does not effect a cure. Many a rider has lost teeth through his horse's head-tossing. As is the case with other behaviour problems, some horses use head-tossing to avoid doing something which does not suit them, or to avoid doing as they are told. Much as it pains me to have to say it, if jabs with the spurs do not help, the horse should be checked sharply with the reins. Shout at the horse – raising the voice is often successful – and check it upwards (not downwards) and towards the opposite shoulder.

Do not forget, as with the previous habit of opening the mouth, to check what you are doing with your hands. All too frequently it is the rider's hand which the horse is objecting to. Also check the fitting and condition of the bit (often bits are fitted too high in the mouth, or too low so that they are resting on the tushes); and do not forget to get the horse's lips and teeth checked, if possible by a vet. You should also consider whether the tossing is caused by the saddle or bridle, for example an over-tight browband pinching the ears, the headpiece pressing on bristles of mane where the rider has cut a piece of hair out (a common but senseless practice), or friction or pressure from buckles. If the head-tossing is caused by constraint in the jaw region, this will present a real problem for the average rider. Where, for example, a ewe neck is accompanied by narrow, or indeed over-broad jaws in which the jaw bones extend too far back, the parotid glands can only function with difficulty, and the horse will always have a tendency to go above the bit.

Swishing the tail

The way a horse carries its tail gives an insight into both its physical and its mental state. The horse's disposition, the amount of energy it has, its constitution, its nervous state, and any tension, will be expressed by the carriage and behaviour of the tail.

Normally the tail moves freely, in rhythm with the stride, with the tip winging from side to side, coinciding with the change of supporting leg. If the tail does not swing rhythmically with the movement, this means that the horse is not moving freely: it is tense. The tail is therefore an infallible guide as to whether and to what extent the horse is working through its back. A horse may be tense on one side, it may not go into the hand on one side, or it may be tired. A horse which carries its tail crookedly may not necessarily have done so from birth. The crookedness may be due to tension. Usually the crookedness disappears at an extended canter, i.e. when the horse is really using itself. Horses born with crooked tails can be helped by surgery. However, there have been cases where cutting one of the dock muscles has been successful to start with, but the crookedness has reappeared later.

Conscious or subconscious misuse of the spur can also cause the tail to react. Mares in particular frequently react to tickling spurs by swishing and lashing with their tails. Mares which do this will have little chance of success in dressage. Swishing and lashing the tail as a sign of inner or outer tension is a problem which will keep cropping up throughout the horse's training. A horse which is doing this is not focusing its attention fully on its rider. The whip should be used, instead of the spurs, on horses which are not very forward going, and which swish their tails.

Clamping the tail down is a practice which is often found in nervous horses which are afraid of being punished. It can also be a sign that the horse is about to kick. If they do it under saddle, for whatever reason, it means that they are not free of constraint, *losgelassen*: the back muscles are not working sufficiently, and neither is the muscle which raises the tail, and which works in conjunction with the back muscles.

Kicking against the spur

There are two forms of kicking against the spur. A particularly sensitive horse which reacts against either intentional or unintentional use of the spur is only too right to do so. It is always the rider's lack of skill which is to blame for this habit. The rider must check his seat, improve his knee and lower leg position and not let his toes turn outwards. The spurs may also be too long, too high or too sharp. Ticklish mares, and mares on heat are particularly sensitive to the spur and should be ridden with a whip.

Some horses are sluggish, and either simply do not want to use themselves or cannot, or will not do so, because, for example, their hind legs are stiff. If the rider decides to reinforce his leg aid with the spur, when the horse is not obeying the sideways-pushing leg behind the girth, he often applies the leg (and spur) even further back, in the area behind the false ribs. In this position it does not serve to make the hind leg step further forward: the horse's only possible reaction is to kick against it. The sensitive abdominal wall further back from the position where the leg normally lies is not supported by the false ribs, and has no connection with the abdominal muscles which swing the hind leg forward. The point at which these muscles can be influenced into contracting lies underneath the leg when the latter is in the normal position, that is, just behind the girth.

The spurs should therefore be applied just behind the girth, and with lazy horses which kick against it, it should be backed up with the whip. Nothing ruins a horse more, or makes it more stubborn, than too frequent and unnecessary use of the spurs. Resistant (restive) horses will only be made worse by it and some horses fly into a rage, dash themselves against the wall or simply lie down. Provided there is nothing constitutionally wrong with them, these horses should be dealt with as explained already at the beginning of the book: their forward urge and their pleasure in their work with the rider must be restored, and the demands made on them must be reduced, so that they are not asked to do anything they are not capable of. If possible, they should be hacked out frequently for a while, and just allowed to potter about with minimum demands being made on them. The rider should judge by feel what the horse is ready for.

Kicking

Just a few points about kicking under saddle to supplement the chapter about kicking against the spur. Owners of kickers are to be pitied: they may be harming people in themselves, but the dislike directed against their horse will also be aimed at them. This is certainly unfair, because there is no completely effective cure for horses which kick when ridden. The best of riders cannot prevent his horse lashing out sometimes when in a group or any kind of equestrian gathering. The best course of action is to protect yourself or other people from being kicked, and to keep your distance at all costs. It has already been pointed out that in the hunting field a kicker can be recognised by a red ribbon on its tail. However, there are times when it is simply not possible to keep the necessary distance from a kicker, and although many of the accidents which happen (usually with unfortunate consequences) could have been avoided, there are many others which occur in spite of the most scrupulous precautions. Kickers do not necessarily kick all the time. When they kick depends on their nature and on whether they do so for food, for sexual reasons, or because they feel generally disagreeable. Kicking may also be a 'one off' occurrence: the horse has never done it before and it never does it again. A habitual kicker, on the other hand, will kick anything – man or beast, or even objects. There is little point in punishing such horses since, as we have seen in the chapter on 'Kicking' in the stable vices section, it may be a reflex action, i.e. something the horse does completely subconsciously. Horses which give some indication that they are about to kick, by making obvious threatening gestures such as laying back the ears, baring the teeth or pushing their quarters towards the object of their dislike, can be corrected accordingly (provided the rider recognises the symptoms in time), by sharply raising the head and neck, transferring as much weight as possible onto the quarters, or leaning right back. Any punishment must be given immediately.

One more thing: when you are out hacking, never shake hands with other riders. Even if you know the horse well, it is better not to, as all sorts of things have been known to happen when horses get this close. Raise your cap and keep your distance.

Epilogue

In this book an attempt has been made to bring together information which may be useful for the handling and use of the horse. We mentioned at the beginning of the book that when the horse ceased to be used intensively, much of the knowledge which was taken for granted was lost, and that now there are necessarily, fewer people about who have a 'feel' for the way a horse behaves ('horse sense'). On the other hand, research into behaviour has increased in importance in recent years. Mention of this subject is no longer greeted with a sympathetic smile, and it is no longer considered to be a rather undemanding science. At least the seeds have been sown for a greater concern with the psychological welfare of our animals. In fact everyone who is intensively involved with horses should make their own small contribution in the field of behaviour research, simply because this broad subject has yet to be explored fully.

Every rider and horsekeeper should be constantly aware of the fact that modern methods of horse keeping entail a basic restriction of the horse's life-style which verges on imprisonment. On the other hand we should not 'humanise' the behavioural characteristics of our charges, but should try instead to discover, from our knowledge of the equine mentality, how a horse would feel. We should be conscious of the fact that the horse was certainly not created by nature to be ridden, to be jumped over very demanding fences, or to perform dozens of changes of leg at canter. If it is to be asked to perform exercises which go beyond the norm, the rider must learn to deal with it correctly from a psychological point of view – from the point of view of equine psychology, that is. This is a broad subject, and there is still a lot to be done and a lot to be said on it. Remember one important point, however: intelligence sensitivity, disposition and other characteristics have nothing to do with whether the horse is a thoroughbred or a pony.

Horses are all different. There are therefore no hard and fast rules for dealing with problems. It only remains for me to wish you every success!

124